IAN HAMILTON'S MARCH

IAN HAMILTON'S MARCH

WINSTON S. CHURCHILL

WILDSIDE PRESS

IAN HAMILTON'S MARCH

Published in 2007 by Wildside Press.
www.wildsidepress.com

THIS COLLECTION OF LETTERS IS INSCRIBED
TO
LIEUT.-GENERAL IAN HAMILTON,
C.B., D.S.O.
WITH WHOSE MILITARY ACHIEVEMENTS
IT IS LARGELY CONCERNED

CONTENTS

MAPS AND PLANS

PREFACE

This book is a continuation of those letters to the *Morning Post* newspaper on the South African War, which have been lately published under the title "London to Ladysmith via Pretoria". Although the letters had been read to some extent in their serial form, their reproduction in a book has been indulgently regarded by the public; and I am encouraged to repeat the experiment.

The principle event with which the second series deals is the march of Lieutenant-General Ian Hamilton's column on the flank of Lord Robert's main army from Bloemfontein to Pretoria. This force, which, far from the railway, marched more than 400 miles through the most fertile parts of the enemy's country, which fought ten general actions and fourteen smaller affairs, and captured five towns, was, owing to the difficulties in telegraphing, scarcely attended by a single newspaper correspondent, and accompanied continuously by none. Little has therefore been heard of its fortunes, nor do I know of anyone who is likely to write an account.

The letters now submitted to the public find in these facts their chief claim to be reprinted. While written in the style of personal narrative I have hitherto found it convenient to follow, they form a complete record of the operations of the flank column from the day when Ian Hamilton left Bloemfontein to attack the Waterworks position, until he returned to Pretoria after the successful engagement of Diamond Hill.

Although in an account written mainly in the field, and immediately after the actual events, there must be mistakes, no care has been spared in the work. The whole book has been diligently revised. Four letters, which our long marches did not allow me to finish while with the troops, have been added and are now published for the first time. The rest have been lengthened or corrected by the light of after-knowledge and reflection, and although the epistolary form remains, I hope the narrative will be found to be fairly consecutive.

I do not want the reader to think that the personal incidents and adventures described in this book are extraordinary, and beyond the common lot of those who move unrestricted about the field of war. They are included in the narrative, not on account of any peculiar or historic interest, but because this method is the easiest, and, so far as my wit serves me, the best way of telling the story with due regard at once to detail and proportion.

In conclusion I must express my obligations to the proprietors of the *Morning Post* newspaper for the assistance they have given my publishers in allowing them to set up the copy as each letter arrived from the war; to the DUKE OF MARLBOROUGH, to whom I am indebted for the details of the strength and composition of the force which will be found in the Appendix, and for much assistance in the attempt to attain accuracy; and thirdly, to MR. FRANKLAND, whose manly record of the heavy days he passed as a prisoner in Pretoria may help to make this book acceptable to the public.

WINSTON S. CHURCHILL

LONDON
September 10, 1900

CHAPTER ONE

A ROVING COMMISSION

In the train near Pieters, Natal: March 31, 1900

Ladysmith, her garrison and her rescuers, were still recovering, the one from the effects of long confinement, the other from over-exertion. All was quiet along the Tugela except for the plashing of the waters, and from Hunger's Poort to Weenen no sound of rifle or cannon shot disturbed the echoes.

The war had rolled northward: the floods of invasion that had isolated — almost overwhelmed — Ladysmith and threatened to submerge the whole country had abated and receded, so that the Army of Natal might spread itself out to feed and strengthen at its leisure and convenience on the re-conquered territory.

Knox's (Ladysmith) Brigade went into camp at Arcadia, five miles west of the town. Howard's (Ladysmith) Brigade retired to the breezy plains south of Colenso. Clery's Division — for the gallant Clery, recovered from sickness, had displaced the gallant and successful Lyttelton — moved north and encamped beyond Elandslaagte along the banks of Sunday's River. Hunter's Division was disposed with one brigade at Elandslaagte and one at Tinta Inyoni. Warren, whom it was no longer necessary to send to the Cape Colony, established himself and his two brigades north of Ladysmith, along the railway line to the Orange Free State. Brocklehurst, with the remnants of what had once been almost a Cavalry Division, and now could scarcely mount three squadrons, occupied a neighbouring plain, sending his regiments one by one to Colenso, or even Mooi River, to be re-horsed; and around all this great Army, resting after its labours and preparing for fresh efforts, the Cavalry brigades of Dundonal and Burn-Murdock drew an immense curtain of pickets and patrols which extended from Acton Homes in the east, through Bester's Station right round to Wessel's Nek and further still, and which enabled the protected soldiers within to close their eyes at night and stretch their legs by day.

Meanwhile, the burghers had all retreated to the Drankensberg and the Biggarsberg and other refuges, from which elevated positions they defied intrusion or attack, and their scattered line stretched in a vast crescent even around our widely extended front from the Tintwa Pass, through Waschbank to Pomeroy.

But with the exception of outpost skirmishes, wholly unimportant to those not engaged in them, a strange peace brooded over Natal, and tranquility was intensified by the recollection of the struggle that was over and the anticipation of the struggle that impended. It was a lull in the storm.

All this might be war, but it was not journalism. The tempest for the moment had passed, and above the army in Natal the sky was monotonously blue. It was true that dark clouds hung near the northern horizon, but who should say when they would break? Not, at any rate, for three weeks, I thought, and so resolved to fill the interval by trying to catch a little of the tempest elsewhere.

After the relief of Ladysmith four courses offered themselves to Sir Redvers Buller. To stand strictly on the defensive in Natal and to send Lord Roberts every man and gun who could be spared; to break into the Free State by forcing Van Reenen's Pass or the Tintwa; to attack the twelve thousand Boers in the Biggarsberg, clear Natal, and invade the Transvaal through the Vryheid district; and, lastly, to unite and reorganise and co-operate with Lord Robert's main advance either by striking west or north.

Which course would be adopted? I made inquires. Staff officers, bland and inscrutable — it is wonderful how well men can keep secrets they have not been told — continued to smile and smile. Brigadiers frankly confessed their ignorance. The general-in-chief observed pleasantly that he would "go for" the enemy as soon as he was ready, but was scarcely precise about when and where.

It was necessary to go to more humble sources for truth, and after diligent search I learned from a railway porter, or somebody like that, that all attempts to repair the bridge across the Sunday's River had been postponed indefinitely. This, on further inquiry, proved to be true.

Now, what does this mean? It means, I take it, that no direct advance against the Biggarsberg is intended for some time; and as the idea of reducing the Natal Army to reinforce the Cape Colony forces has been definitely abandoned, the western line of advance suggests itself.

It would be absurd to force Van Reenen's Pass with heavy loss of life, when by waiting until the main army has reached, let us say, Kroonstad, we could walk through without opposition: so that it looks very likely that the Natal troops will do nothing until Lord Robert's advance is more developed, and that then they will enter the Free State and operate in conjunction with him, all of which is strategy and common sense besides. At any rate there will be a long delay.

Therefore, I said to myself, I will go to Bloemfontein, see all that may be seen there and on the way, and rejoin the Natal Army when it comes through the passes. Such was the plan, and the reader shall be witness to its abandonment.

I left the camp of Dundonald's Brigade early in the morning of the 29th of March, and riding through Ladysmith, round the hill on which stands the battered convent, now serving as headquarters, and down the main street, along which the relieving Army had entered the city, reached the railway station and caught the 10 a.m. down train.

We were delayed for a few minutes by the departure for Elands-laagte of a train load of Volunteers, the first to reach the Natal Army, and the officers hastened to look at these citizen soldiers. There were five companies in all, making nearly a thousand men, fine-looking fellows, with bright intelligent eyes, which they turned inquiringly on every object in turn, pointing and laughing at the numerous shell holes in the corrugated iron engine sheds and other buildings of the station.

A few regulars — sunburnt men, who had fought their way in with Buller — sauntered up to the trucks, and began a conversation with the reinforcement. I caught a fragment: "Cattle trucks, are they? Well, they didn't give us no blooming cattle trucks. No, no! We came into Ladysmith in a first-class doubly extry Pullman car. 'Oo sent 'em? Why, President —— Kruger, of course," whereat there was much laughter.

I must explain that the epithet which the average soldier uses so often as to make it perfectly meaningless, and which we conveniently express by a ——, is always placed immediately before the noun it is intended to qualify. For instance, no solider would under any circumstances say "—— Mr. Kruger has pursued a —— reactionary policy," but "Mr. —— Kruger has pursued a reactionary —— policy." Having once voyaged for five days down the Nile in a sailing boat with a company of Grenadiers, I have had the best opportunities for being acquainted with these idiomatic constructions, and I insert this little note in case it may be useful to some of our national poets and minstrels.

The train started across the well-known ground, and how fast and easily it ran. Already we were bounding through the scrub in which a month before Dundonald's leading squadrons, galloping in with beating hearts, had met the hungry picket line.

Intombi Spruit hospital camp was reached in a quarter of an hour. Hospital camp no longer, thank goodness! Since the bridge had been repaired the trains had been busy, and two days before I left the town the last of the 2,500 sick had been moved down to the great hospital and convalescent camps at Mooi River and Highlands, or on to the ships in the Durban Harbour. Nothing remained behind but 100 tents and marquees, a stack of iron cots, the cook houses, the drinking-water tanks, and 600 graves. Ghastly Intombi had faded into the past, as a nightmare flies at the dawn of day.

We sped swiftly across the plain of Pieters, and I remembered how I had toiled across it, some five months before, a miserable captive, casting longing eyes at the Ladysmith balloon, and vigilantly guarded by the Boer mounted escort. Then the train ran into the deep ravine between Barton's Hill and Railway Hill, the ravine the cavalry had "fanned" on the day of the battle, and, increasing its pace as we descended towards the Tugela, carried us along the whole front of the Boer position. Signs of the fighting appeared on every side. Biscuit tins flashed brightly on the hillside like heliographs. In places the slopes were honeycombed with little stone walls and traverses, masking the sheltering refuges of the infantry battalions during the week they had lain in the sun-blaze exposed to the cross-fire of gun and rifle. White wooden crosses gleamed here and there among the thorn bushes. The dark lines of the Boer trenches crowned the hills. The train swept by — and that was all.

I knew every slope, every hillock and accident of ground, as one knows men and women in the world. Here was good cover. There was a dangerous space. Here it was wise to stoop, and there to run. Behind that steep kopje a man might scorn the shrapnel. Those rocks gave sure protection from the flanking rifle fire. Only a month ago how much these things had meant. If we could carry that ridge it would command those trenches, and that might mean the hill itself, and perhaps the hill would lead to Ladysmith. Only a month ago these things meant honour or shame, victory or defeat, life or death. An anxious Empire and a waiting world wanted to know about every one of them — and now they were precisely what I have said, dark jumbled mounds of stone and scrub, with a few holes and crevices scratched in them, and a litter of tin pots, paper, and cartridge-cases strewn about.

The train steamed cautiously over the temporary wooden bridge at Colenso and ran into the open country beyond. On we hurried past the green slope where poor Long's artillery had been shot to bits, past Gun Hill, whence the great naval guns had fired so often, through Chieveley Camp, or rather through the site of Chieveley Camp, past the wreck of the armoured train — still lying where we had dragged it with such labour and peril, just clear of the line —

through Frere and Estcourt, and so, after seven hours' journey, we came to Pietermaritzburg.

An officer who was travelling down with me pointed out the trenches on the signal hill above the town.

"Seems queer," he said, "to think that the Boers might so easily have taken this town. When we dug those trenches they were expected every day; and the Governor, who refused to leave the capital and was going to stick it out with us, had his kit packed ready to come up into the entrenchments at an hour's notice."

It was very pleasant to know that those dark and critical days were gone, and that the armies in the field were strong enough to maintain the Queen's dominions against any further invasion; yet one could not but recall with annoyance that the northern part of Natal was still in the hands of the enemy. Not for long, however, shall this endure.

After waiting in Pietermaritzburg long enough only to dine, I proceeded by the night train to Durban, and was here so fortunate as to find a Union boat, the *Guelph*, leaving almost immediately for East London. The weather was fine, the sea comparatively smooth, and the passengers few and unobtrusive, so that the voyage, being short, might almost be considered pleasant.

The captain took the greatest interest in the war, which he had followed with attention, and with the details and incidents of which he was extraordinarily familiar. He had brought out a ship full of volunteers, new drafts, and had much to say concerning the British soldier and his comrades in arms.

The good news which had delighted and relieved everyone had reached him in the most dramatic and striking manner. When they left England Roberts had just begun his welcome advance, and the public anxiety was at its height. At Madeira there was an English cable to say that he was engaging Cronje, and that no news had arrived for three days. This was supplied, however, by the wire, which asserted with circumstantial details that the British had been heavily defeated and had fled south beyond the Orange River. With this to reflect on, they had to sail. Imagine the doubts and fears that flourished in ten days of ignorance, idleness, and speculation. Imagine with what feelings they approached St. Helena. He told me that when the tug boat came off no man dared hail them for news. Nor was it until the launch was alongside that a soldier cried out nervously, "The war, the war: what's happened there!" and when they heard the answer, "Cronje surrendered; Ladysmith relieved," he said that such a shout went up as he had never heard before, and I believed him.

After twenty-four hours of breeze and tossing the good ship found herself in the roads at East London, and having by this time had quite enough of the sea I resolved to disembark forthwith.

CHAPTER TWO

EXIT GENERAL GATACRE

Bethany: April 13, 1900

If you go to sleep when the train leaves East London, you should wake, all being well, to find yourself at Queenstown.

Queenstown lies just beyond the high-water mark of war. The tide had flowed strong after Stormberg, and it looked as if Queenstown would be engulfed, at any rate for a time. But Fortune and General Gatacre protected it. Sterkstroom entrenched itself, and prepared for daily attacks. Molteno was actually shelled. Queenstown suffered none of the horrors of war except martial law, which it bore patiently rather than cheerfully.

Nothing in the town impressed the traveller, but at the dining-room of the railway station there was a very little boy, about twelve years old, who, unaided, managed to serve, with extraordinary despatch and a grand air, a whole score of passengers during the brief interval allowed for refreshments.

Five months earlier I had passed along this line, hoping to get into Ladysmith before the door was shut, and had been struck by this busy child, who seemed a product of American rather than of Africa. Much had happened in the meantime, not so far from where he lived. But here he was still — the war had not interfered with him, Queenstown was beyond the limit.

At Sterkstroom a line of empty trenches, the Red Cross flag over a hospital, and an extension to the cemetery enclosure filled with brown mounds which the grass had not yet had time to cover, showed that we had crossed the line between peace and war. Passing through Molteno, the last resting-place of the heroic de Montmorency, the train reached Stormberg. Scarcely any traces of the Boer occupation were to be seen; the marks of their encampment behind the ridge where they had laagered — a litter of meat tins, straw, paper, and the like, the grave of Commandant Swanepoole and several nameless heaps, a large stone (in the stationmaster's possession) with the words engraved on it: "In memory of the Transvaal commando, Stormberg, December 1899", and that was all. The floods had abated and receded. This was the only jetsam that remained.

At Stormberg I changed my mind, or, rather — for it comes to the same thing and sounds better — I made it up.

I heard that no immediate advance from Bloemfontein was likely or even possible for a fortnight. Therefore, I said, I will go to Capetown, and shelter for a week at "The Helot's Rest". After all, what is the use of a roving commission if one cannot rove at random or caprice?

So to Capetown I went accordingly — seven hundred miles in forty-eight hours of bad trains over sections of the lie only newly reopened. But Capetown at this present time is not an edifying place. Yet, since one may be curious to know some reason for such advice, let me explain.

Capetown, which stands, as some writers have observed, beneath the shadow of Table Mountain, has been — and may be again in times of peace — a pleasant place in which to pursue business or health; but now it is simply a centre of intrigue, scandal, falsehood, and rumor.

The visitor stays at the Mount Nelson Hotel, if he can be so fortunate as to secure a room. At this establishment he finds all the luxuries of a first-class European hotel without the resulting comfort. There is a good dinner, but it is cold before it reaches him; there is a spacious dining-room, but it is overcrowded; there are clean European waiters, but they are few and far between.

At the hotel, in its garden, or elsewhere in the town, all the world and his wife are residing — particularly the wife.

We used to think, in the Army of Natal, that Lord Robert's operations in the Free State had been a model of military skill and knowledge, and, in a simple way, we regarded French as one of the first cavalry soldiers of the age.

All this was corrected at Capetown, and I learned with painful disenchantment that "it" (the said operation) had all been a shameful muddle from beginning to end; that the Field-Marshal had done this and that and the other "which no man in his senses", &c., that French was utterly . . . and as for Lord Kitchener, Capetown — let us be just, imported social Capetown   was particularly severe on Lord Kitchener.

It was very perplexing; and besides it seemed that these people ought to know, for they succeeded in making more news in the twenty-four hours than all the correspondents at the front put together. The whole town was overrun with amateur strategists and gossiping women. There were more colonels to the acre than in any place outside the United States, and if the social aspect was unattractive, the political was scarcely more pleasing.

Party feeling ran high. Some of the British section, those tremendous patriots who demonstrate but do not fight — not to be on any account compared with the noble fellows who fill the volunteer corps — pot-house heroes, and others of that kidney, had just distinguished themselves by mobbing Mr. Schreiner in the streets.

The Dutch section, some of them the men who, risking nothing themselves, had urged the Republics to their ruin, all of whom had smiled and rubbed their hands at the British reverses, sat silent in public, but kept a strict watch on incoming steamers for members of Parliament and others of more influence than guile, and whispered honeyed assurances of their devotion to the Empire, coupled with all sorts of suggestions about the settlement — on the broad general principle of "Heads I win, tails you lose".

British newspapers advocated short shrift to rebels — "Hit 'em hard now they're down"; "Give them a lesson this time, the dirty Dutchmen!" Dutch papers recorded the events of the war in the tone, "At the end of the battle the British, as usual fled precipitately, leaving 2,000 killed, *our* loss" — no, not quite that, but very nearly; everything, in fact, but the word "our" — "one killed, two slightly wounded."

Let no one stay long in Capetown now who would carry away a true impression of the South Africans. There is too much shoddy worn there at present.

Only at Government House did I find the Man of No Illusion, the anxious but unwearied Proconsul, understanding the faults and the virtues of both sides, measuring the balance of rights and wrongs, and determined — more determined than even; for is it not the only hope for the future of South Africa? — to use his knowledge and his power to strengthen the Imperial ties.

All this time the reader has been left on a siding at Naauwpoort; but does he complain of not being taken to Capetown? We will hasten back together to the healthier atmosphere of war.

Indeed, the spell of the great movement impending in the Free State began to catch hold of me before I had travelled far on the line towards Bloemfontein. Train loads of troops filled every station or siding. A ceaseless stream of men, horses, and guns had been passing northwards for a fortnight, and on the very day that I made the journey Lord Kitchener had ordered that in future all troops must march beyond Springfontein, because the line must be cleared for the passage of supplies, so that, besides the trains in the sidings, there were columns by the side of the railway steadily making their way to the front.

The one passenger train in the day stopped at Bethany. I got out. To go on was to reach Bloemfontein at midnight. Better, then, to sleep here and proceed at dawn.

"Are there many troops here?" I asked. They replied, "The whole of the Third Division." "Who commands?" "Gatacre." That decided me.

I knew the general slightly, having made his acquaintance up the Nile in pleasant circumstances, for no one was allowed to pass his mess hungry or thirsty. I was very anxious to see him and hear all about Stormberg and the rest of the heavy struggle along the eastern line of rail. I found him in a tin house close to the station. He received me kindly, and we had a long talk. The General explained to me many things which I had not understood before, and after we had done with past events he turned with a hopeful eye to the future. At last, and for the first time, he was going to have the division of which he had originally been given the command.

"You know I only had two and a half battalions at Sterkstroom and a few colonial horse; but now I have got both my brigades complete."

I thought him greatly altered from the dashing, energetic man I had known up the river, or had heard about on the frontier or in plague-stricken Bombay. Four months of anxiety and abuse had left their mark on him. The weary task of keeping things going with utterly insufficient resources, and in the face of an adroit and powerful enemy in a country of innumerable kopjes, where every advantage lay with the Boer, had bowed that iron frame and tired the strange energy which had made him so remarkable among soldiers. But when he thought of the future his face brightened. The dark days were over. The broken rocky wilderness lay behind, and around rolled the grassy plains of the Free State. He had his whole division at least. Moreover, there was prospect of immediate action. So I left him, for it was growing late, and went my way. Early next morning he was dismissed from his command and ordered to England, broken, ruined, and disgraced.

I will not for a moment dispute the wisdom or the justice of his removal. In stormy weather one must trust to the man at the helm, and when he is such a man as Lord Roberts it is not a very hard thing to do. But because General Gatacre has been cruelly persecuted in England by people quite ignorant of the difficulties of war or of the conditions under which it is carried on in this country, it is perhaps not out of place to write a few words of different tenor.

Gatacre was a man who made his way in the army, not through any influence or favour which he enjoyed, but by sheer hard work and good service. Wherever he had served he had left a high record behind him. On the Indian frontier he gained the confidence of so fine a soldier as Sir Bindon Blood, and it was largely to his reputation won in the Chitral Expedition that his subsequent advancement was due. At Bombay in 1897 he was entrusted with the duty of fighting the plague, then first gripping its deadly fingers into the city. No one who is at all acquainted with the course of this pest will need to be told how excellent was his work. After the last Soudan campaign I travelled from Bombay to Poona with a Parsee gentleman, a wealthy merchant of the plague-stricken town, and I well remember how he dilated on the good which Gatacre had done.

"He was our only chance," said the black man. "Now he is gone, and the sickness will stay for ever."

Gatacre's part in the Soudan campaign has been described at length elsewhere. His courage has never been questioned, because the savage critics did not wish to damage their cause by obvious absurdities. If I were to discuss his tactics in the Boer war here I should soon get on the ground which I have forbidden myself. It is sufficient to observe that Gatacre retained the confidence and affection of his soldiers in the most adverse circumstances. When the weary privates struggled back to camp after the disastrous day at Stormberg they were quite clear on one point: "No one could have got us out but him." Two days before he was dismissed the Cameron Highlanders passed through Bethany, and the men recognized the impetuous leader of the Atbara charge; and, knowing he had fallen among evil days, cheered him in the chivalry of the common man. The poor general was much moved at this spontaneous greeting, which is a very rare occurrence in our phlegmatic, well-ordered British Army. Let us hope the sound will long ring in his ears, and, as it were, light a bright lamp of memory in the chill and dreary evening of life.

Exit General Gatacre. "Now," as my Parsee merchant remarked, "he is gone"; and I suppose there are, here and there, notes of triumph. But among them I will strike a note of warning. If the War Office breaks generals not so much for incapacity as for want of success with any frequency, it will not find men to fight for it in brigade and divisional commands. Every man who knows the chances of war feels himself insecure. The initiative which an unsympathetic discipline has already killed, or nearly killed, in younger officers, will wither and die in their superiors. You will have generals as before, but they will not willingly risk the fruits of long years of service in damnable countries and of perils of all to divide responsibility. They will ask for orders or instructions. But they will not fight — if they can possibly help it, and then only on the limited liability principle, which means the shedding of much blood without any result. Besides, as an irreverent subaltern remarked to me: "If you begin with Gatacre, where are you going to end? What about poor old —— ?"

But I dare not pursue the subject further.

CHAPTER THREE

AT HALF-WAY HOUSE

Bloemfontein: April 16, 1900

After a decent interval let the curtain rise on a new act.
The scene and most of the characters are different, but it
is same play. The town — a town of brick and tin — stands at the apparent edge of a vast plain of withered grass, from whose inhospi-
table aspect it turns and nestles, as if for protection, round the
scrub-covered hills to northward. From among the crowd of one-
storied dwelling-houses, more imposing structures, the seats of
Government and commerce, rise prominently to catch the eye and
impress the mind with the pleasing prospect of wealthier civilisation. Here and there are towers and pinnacles, and, especially
remarkable, a handsome building surrounded in the classic style by
tall white pillars and, surmounted by a lofty dome, looks like a Parliament House, but for the Red Cross flag which flies from the
summit and proclaims that, whatever may have been its former purposes, the spacious hall within is at last devoted to the benefit of
mankind. The dark hills — their uncertain outline marked at one
point by the symmetrical silhouette of a fort — form the background of the picture: Bloemfontein, April, 1900.

It is five o'clock in the afternoon. The Market-square is
crowded with officers and soldiers listening to the band of the
Buffs. Every regiment in the service, every Colony in the Empire is
represented; all clad in uniform khaki, but distinguished by an
extraordinary variety of badges.

Each group is a miniature system of Imperial Federation. The
City Volunteer talks to a Queensland Mounted Infantryman, who
hands his matchbox to a private of the Line. A Bushman from New
Zealand, a Cambridge undergraduate, and a tea-planter from Ceylon stroll up and make the conversation general. On every side all
kinds of men are intermingled, united by the sympathy of a common purpose and soldered together in the fire of war. And this will
be of great consequence later on.

The inhabitants — bearded burghers who have made their
peace, townsfolk who never desired to make a quarrel — stand
round and watch complacently. After all, there are worse things
than to be defeated. Demand is keen, the army is wealthy, and prices
are high. Trade has followed hard on the flag which waves from

every building; and, whether it be for merchandise or farm produce, the market is buoyant.

The officers congregate about the pretentious building of the club, and here I find acquaintances gathered together from all the sentry beats of the Empire, for the regular army usually works like a kaleidoscope and, new combinations continually forming, scatter old friends in every direction. But here all are collected once more, and the man we met on the frontier, the man we met "up the river", the man we met at manœuvres with the comrade of Sandhurst, the friend or enemy of Harrow days, and the rival of a Meerut tournament, stand in a row together. Merry military music, laughing faces, bright, dainty little caps, a moving throng, and the consciousness that this means a victorious British Army in the capital of the Free State, drive away all shadows from the mind.

One cannot see any gaps in the crowd; it is so full of animation that the spaces where Death has put his hand are not to be seen. The strong surges of life have swept across them as a sunny sea closes over a foundered ship. Yet they are not quite forgotten.

"Hullo, my dear old boy, I am glad to see you. When did you get up here? Have you brought ___ with you? Oh, I am sorry. It must have been a fever-stricken hole, that Ladysmith. Poor chap! Do you remember how he . . . Charlie has gone home. He can never play polo again — expanding bullet smashed his arm all to bits. Bad luck, wasn't it? Now we've got to find a new back . . . and ___ was killed at Paardeberg . . . spoiled the whole team." The band struck into a lively tune. "How long is it going to last?"

"With luck it ought to be over by October, just a year from start to finish."

"I thought you said something about Pretoria the third week in March."

"Ah, I must have meant May, or perhaps, June."

"Or August."

"Who can tell? But I think this is the half-way house."

The conversation stops abruptly. Everyone looks round. Strolling across the middle of the square, quite alone, was a very small grey-haired gentleman, with extremely broad shoulders and a most unbending back. He wore a staff cap with a broad red band and a heavy gold-laced peak, brown riding boots, a tightly-fastened belt, and no medals, orders, or insignia of any kind. But no one doubted his identity for an instant, and I knew that I was looking at the Queen's greatest subject, the commander who had in the brief space of a month revolutionised the fortunes of war, had turned disaster into victory, and something like despair into almost inordinate triumph.

Other soldiers of career and quality mingled with the diversified throng. Macdonald sits on a bay pony near the club verandah talking to Martyr of the Mounted Infantry and of Central African repute. Pole-Carew, who came to the Cape as Sir Redvers Buller's camp commander, and passed at a bound to brigadier-general, and by another still greater leap to the command of the Eleventh Division, canters across the square. General French and his staff have just ridden up. But the central figure holds all eyes, and everyone knows that it is on him, and him alone, that the public fortunes depend.

Such was the scene on the afternoon of my arrival in Bloemfontein. What of the situation? The first thing to be done after the occupation of the town was to re-open the railway. The presence of a large army in their rear and the swift advance of Gatacre and Clements compelled the invaders to withdraw from Cape Colony, so that Norval's Point and Bethulie bridges were once more in British hands. Both were, however, destroyed or partially destroyed. Besides these, various other smaller bridges and culverts had been blown up. All these were forthwith repaired by the engineers, and through communication by rail was established between the advanced Field Army in the Free State and the sea bases at East London, Port Elizabeth, and Capetown.

In the meantime the army at Bloemfontein lived on the reserve of rations it had carried from Modder River. When the railway was opened the line from Modder River was dropped. A broad-gauge railway, even though it be only a single line, is usually capable of supplying an army of at least 50,000 men with considerable ease, and the reader may remember how the Natal Government Railway was able to support 30, 000 men through January and February, to transport reinforcements and sick, and to run all its ordinary traffic in addition. But the repaired or provisional bridges on the Bloemfontein line caused so much delay that the carrying power of the railway was seriously diminished. When a permanent bridge has been blown up two alternatives present themselves to the engineers: a high-level or a low-level substitute. The high-level bridge, such as was thrown across the Tugela after the relief of Ladysmith, takes much longer to build, but, when built, trains are run straight over it with very little diminution of speed. It is, moreover, secure against floods.

The low-level bridge must be approached by zigzag ramps, which impose frequent shuntings, and cause great delay; and it is, of course, only to be trusted when there are no floods. But it has this inestimable advantage in military operations: speed in construction. The army must be fed immediately. So the low-level bridges were chosen; hence an early but reduced supply. When this was further minimised by the passage of reinforcements the commissariat depots could scarcely make headway, but must be content to feed the army from day to day and accumulate at the rate, perhaps, of only one day in three, or even one in four. It was, therefore, evident that no offensive movement to the northward could be made for several weeks.

See how the stomach governs the world. By the rapid invasion of their territories, by the staggering blows which they had been dealt at Kimberley, Paardeberg, Poplar Grove, and Driefontein, and by the bad news from Natal, the Boers in the Free State were demoralised. If we could have pressed them unceasingly the whole country would have been conquered to the Vaal River. Encouraged by Lord Robert's Proclamation, and believing that all resistance in the Southern Republic was at an end, great numbers of Free Staters returned to their homes, took the oath of neutrality, and prepared to accept the inevitable.

But while the army waited, as it was absolutely forced to wait, to get supplies, to get horses — to get thousands of horses — to give the infantry new boots, and all arms in a little breathing space, the Boers recovered from their panic, pulled themselves together, and, for the moment, boldly seized the offensive.

Great, though perhaps temporary, were the advantages which they gained. The belief that the war in the Free State was at an end, which had led so many of the burghers to return to their farms, was shared to some extent by the British commander, and loudly proclaimed by his colonial advisers. To protect the farmers who had made their peace the Imperial forces were widely extended. A line was drawn across the Free State from Fourteen Steams, through Boshof, Bloemfontein, and Thabanchu, south of which it was assumed that the country was pacified and conquered.

Meanwhile Olivier and the southern commando, recalled from their operations in the Cape Colony, were making a hurried and, as it seemed, a desperate march to rejoin the main Boer forces. They expected the attack of the same terrible army which had already devoured Cronje; nor was it until they reached Ladybrand and found only Pilcher with a few hundred men snapping at their heels that they realised that the bulk of the British troops were for the moment practically immobile at Bloemfontein. Then they turned.

Pilcher fled warily before them, and fell back on Broadwood's Brigade, near Thabanchu. With renewed courage and strong reinforcements from their friends north of the line of occupation they pressed on. Broadwood was compelled to fall back on the Ninth Division, which was camped west of the waterworks. He made a twenty-mile march at night and laagered in the small hours of the morning, thinking, as most people would think, that pursuit was for the time being shaken off. Morning broke, and with it a Boer cannonade.

I do not intend to be drawn into a detailed description of the action that followed. For many reasons it deserves separate and detailed consideration, chiefly because it shows the Boer at his very best: crafty in war and, above all things, deadly cool. In a word, what happened was this: The shells crashed into the laager. Everyone said, "Take the blasted waggons out of the shell fire. We will cover their retreat"; which they did most beautifully: Broadwood displaying all the skill which had enabled him to disentangle the reconnaissance of the 5th of April near the Atbara from the clutches of the Dervishes. The said waggons hurried out of the shell fire only to fall into the frying-pan of an ambuscade. Guns, prisoners and much material fell into the hands of the Boers. The Ninth Division retreated suddenly — too suddenly, say the army, with other remarks which it is not my business to transcribe — on Bloemfontein, and the force of the storm fell on Gatacre.

Gatacre had a post at Dewersdorp: three companies of the Royal Irish Rifles, two of Mounted Infantry. So soon as he heard of the retirement of the Ninth Division he sent orders by many routes for his post to fall back too. They fell back accordingly; but at Reddersburg the net closed around them. Let us judge no man harshly or in ignorance. Fighting followed. With a loss of eight killed and thirty-one wounded, the retreating troops surrendered when relief was scarcely five miles away. Everything curled back on to Bloemfontein and the railway line, which it was *vital* to hold. Reinforcements were thrust to the front to meet the emergency: Rundle, with the Eighth Division was diverted from Kimberley to Springfontein; Hunter, with the Tenth Division (our old friends the Irish and Fusilier Brigades), started from Natal, thus condemning Buller to the strict defensive, and the Boers swept southward.

Now, in accordance with the terms of Lord Roberts's Proclamation, many farmers of the Free State, fighting men of the Boer Army — that is to say, who had thought that all was up: deserters, in other words — had come into the British posts, made their submission, taken the oath, and returned to their farms. The Boers were very angry with these people. What protection could we give them? Some, it is said — it may be a lie — were shot by the enemy. Most of them, from fear or inclination, rejoined their commandos.

The whole of the right-hand bottom corner of the Free State was overrun. Southward still hastened the Boer forces. Brabant was the next to feel the tempest. His garrison in Wepener was assailed, surrounded, fought well — perhaps is now fighting desperately. Other Boers approached the rebel districts of Cape Colony. The lately penitent rebels stirred, are stirring.

Mark, by the way, this sedition is not the result of misplaced generosity but of military misfortunes. No one expects beaten men to be grateful; but, under certain conditions, they will be loyal. An enemy at their throats is not one of those conditions. Southward still sweep the commandos *with empty carts*, for this is the most fertile of all the Republican territories; and, in the meanwhile, what are we doing? Divisions and brigades are being moved by a strong yet deliberate hand. The hope — general and special idea in one — is to catch these bold fellows who have thrust their heads thus far into the lion's mouth and enjoyed until now such immunity. Wepener making a brave defence; Brabant marching through Rouxville to bar their advance; Rundle, Chermiside, and Brabazon striking east from Edenburg to shut the door behind them with two infantry divisions, twenty-four guns, and 2,000 yeomanry; and, further north, the great Bloemfontein Army — four infantry brigades, and many guns — is almost ready to move. Assuredly these Boers are in a dangerous place. Will they escape? Will they, perhaps, carry some part of the intercepting lines with them as a trophy of victory? "Qui vivra verra", and, if these letters continue, "who runs may read", for I purpose to journey via Edenburg to Reddersburg tomorrow, and thence on to the point of collision, which must mark the climax of this extremely interesting event henceforth to be called "The Operations in the Right-hand Bottom Corner of the Free State".

CHAPTER FOUR

TWO DAYS WITH BRABAZON

Before Dewetsdorp: April 21, 1900

When the incursion of the Boers into the recently pacified districts became known, the Eight Division (Rundle) was diverted from Kimberley, whither it was (Chermside, in supersession of Gatacre) massed at Bethany. Still more troops were needed to guard the line and clear the country.

Sir Redvers Buller was asked whether he could co-operate by forcing Van Reenen's Pass and bringing pressure on the enemy's line of retreat. His position in the centre of the triangle of Natal was, however, an inconvenient one. The strategic advantages possessed by the Boers in this scene of the war have before been noticed. But it may be worth while to explain them again.

The enemy possess the superiority of an enveloping frontier. If Sir Redvers Buller moves west through Van Reenen's Pass to make the division required in the Free State, down will come the Boers from the Biggarsberg on his communications and into South Natal. If he moves north to attack the Biggarsberg positions in order to clear Natal he will cut the Boers on his left flank and line.

According to the best information there are three thousand Boers on the Drakensberg Passes, and ten thousand on the Biggarsberg. Buller, therefore, would have preferred to mask Van Reenen's with the Ladysmith Division (Fourth, Lyttelton), which was getting well and strong again, and move northwards with the Second, Fifth, and Tenth Divisions. He did not consider until northern Natal should be cleared that he could safely move westward. On the other hand, the need in the Free State was urgent, and it was therefore arranged that the Tenth Division (Hunter) should come by sea to East London — one brigade to replaced the division diverted from Kimberley, one brigade to Bethulie, and that the rest of the Natal Field Army should remain strictly on the defensive until the situation was materially altered.

Practically, therefore, five brigades of troops were available for the operations in the right-hand bottom corner: Hart, with a brigade of Hunter's Division at Bethulie, the Third and Eighth Divisions under Chermside and Rundle at Springfontein and Bethany. Besides these powerful bodies, which were quite independent of the communication troops or the Bloemfontein Army, there were four-

teen hundred yeomanry and mounted infantry under General Brabazon, and Brabant's Colonial Brigade, about two thousand five
hundred strong.

It is scarcely necessary to follow all the movements in exact
detail. Rundle formed a column at Edenburg, and marching to
Reddersburg, joined his force to part of Chermside's Division from
Bethany, thus having under his immediate command eight battalions, four batteries, and Brabazon's Mounted Brigade. Another brigade was collecting at Edenburg under Campbell. Hart was moved
north-east towards Rouxville, where was also Brabant with a thousand horse. The rest of Brabant's force, some fifteen hundred
strong, were blockaded in Wepener by the enemy. Such was the situation when I left Bloemfontein on the morning of the 17th.

I travelled prosperously; came by rail to Edenburg, trekked
from there in drenching rains, most unusual for this time of year,
and greatly increasing the difficulties of supply; and, resting for the
night at Reddersburg, caught up the marching column in its camp,
about eleven miles from Dewetsdorp, on the night of the 19th.

The position of the various troops was then as follows: Rundle,
with eight battalions, four batteries, and fifteen hundred horse at
Oorlogs Poort, about twelve miles from Dewetsdorp; Campbell,
with two battalions and a battery near Rosendal, marching to join
him; the Grenadier Guards double marching through Reddersburg
to catch up the main force; Hart, with four battalions in Rouxville;
Dalgety, with a garrison of fifteen hundred men, holding Wepener.

So far as could be learned the enemy had about seven thousand
men with twelve guns south of the Bloemfontein-Thabanchu line
under Commandants Olivier and De Wet, and with this force,
which made up in enterprise and activity what it lacked in numbers
or material, they were attempting to blockade and attack Wepener,
to bar the road of Rundle's column to Dewetsdorp, and to check
Brabant and Hart at Smithfield. Besides proposing this ambitious
programme, the Boers sent their patrols riding about the country
commandeering all pacified farmers under threats of death.

We had a very pleasant ride from Reddersburg, and it was evening when we rounded the shoulder of a grassy hill and saw the
camp of the main British column before us. It lay about the foot of a
prominent knoll rising from a broad plain, which was in striking
contrast to the mountains of Natal, and seemed to promise ample
opportunity to the regular soldier. "Camp" is, perhaps, an inaccu-
rate description, for there were scarcely any tents to be seen, and the
rolling ground was littered with swarms of grazing horses and oxen,
and overspread with an immense canopy of white smoke from the

hundreds of gleaming grass fires lighted to cook the soldiers' suppers. I presented myself to Sir Leslie Rundle, who received me courteously, and briefly explained the outlines of the situation. We had arrived in the nick of time. The whole force would march at dawn. The scouts had exchanged shot during the day. The Kaffir spies reported that the enemy would fight on the morrow. What could be better? So with much satisfaction we went to bed.

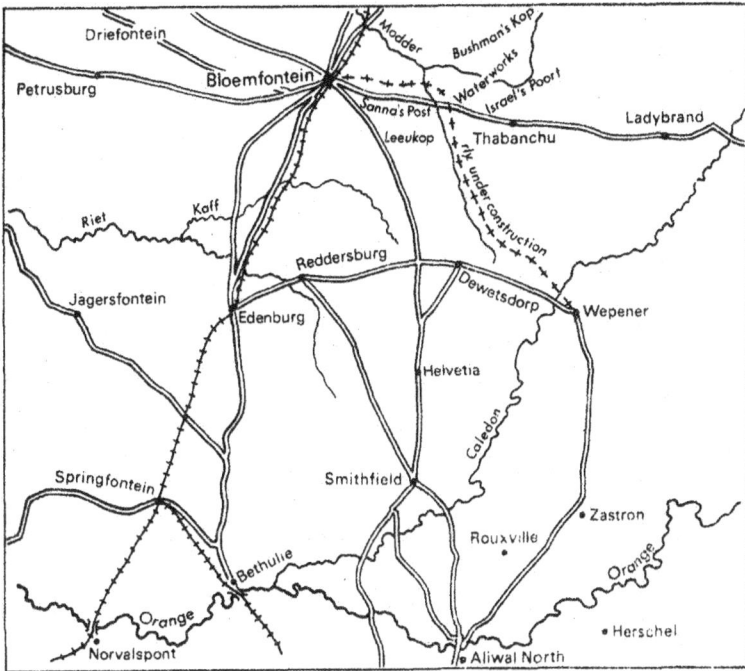

OPERATIONS IN THE O.F.S., APRIL 1900

There was a biting chill in the air when the first light of dawn began to grow in the sky, nor was I the only one who searched a modest kit for some of those warm clothes which our friends at home have thoughtfully been sending out. The South African winter was drawing near. But the sun soon rose, and we shivered no longer. The cavalry were early astir. Indeed their mounted squadrons in silhouette against the morning sky was my first waking impression, and by half-past five all were in motion. I started a little later, but it was not long before I overtook them. Though the command was not a large one, it presented several interesting features.

For the first time I saw the Imperial Yeomanry in the field. Trotting across the beautiful green pasture land in a most extended formation, to which they seemed readily to adapt themselves, were seven hundred yeomen, all good men and true, who had volunteered to fight because they understood the main causes of the quarrel, and from personal conviction earnestly desired to be of some assistance to the State, and who were, moreover, excellently mounted on smart, short-docked cobs, which they sat and rode like the sportsmen they mostly were.

We were moving along in a wide formation, which secured us against all possibilities of surprise, when suddenly I noticed that the scouts far in front were halted.

"Tit-tat, tit-tat": two shots from a high plateau to the right. Shots fired towards you, I must explain, make a double, and those fired away from you a single, report.

We had flushed one of the enemy's outposts. Riding nearer, I could see their figures — seven in all — exposed on the skyline. This showed they were only an outpost, and wished to make us believe they were more. When the Boer is in force he is usually invisible. Still, the position was a strong one, and it is always a possibility worth considering with the Boer that he may foresee your line of thought, and just go one step further, out of contrariness. General Brabazon therefore halted his centre squadrons and detached a turning force of three companies of Yeomanry to the right.

We waited, watching the scouts exchange shots with the Boer picket, and watching — for it was a very pretty sight — the Yeomanry spread out and gallop away to the flank like a pack of hounds in full cry, each independent, yet the whole simultaneous. In a quarter of an hour they were scrambling up the steep sides of the plateau almost in rear of the obstructive picket, which hurriedly departed while time remained. Then the centre swung forward, and the whole cavalry force advanced again, the greater part of it moving on to the plateau, where a running flight with the Dutch outposts now commenced at long range.

Several times we thought that we had unmasked their main position, and that the cavalry work for the day was over, but each time Brabazon's turning movement on the right, the execution of which was entrusted to Colonel Sitwell, a very dashing officer of Egyptian note, compelled them to fall back. After an hour of this sort of thing we were in possession of practically the whole of the plateau, which turned out to be of large extent.

Beyond it, commanding it, essential to it, yet not of it, was a steep rocky kopje. The swift advance and the necessity of pressing the enemy had left the infantry a long way behind. The General felt, however, that this point must be secured. McNeill made a dash for it with the scouts. The yeomanry galloped off to the right again, as if about to surround it, and the Boers allowed themselves to be bounced out of this strong and important position, and scampered away to a smooth green hill a mile in rear. Brabazon made haste to occupy the captured kopje in force, and did so just in time, for as soon as the turning force — two companies (I am going to call them squadrons in the future) of yeomanry and a company of mounted infantry — approached the green hill, the musketry suddenly grew from an occasional drip into a regular patter, and there was the loud boom of a field gun. We had found the main Boer position, and the cavalry came to a standstill.

The enemy now directed a very sharp fire on the captured kopje, which, it seems, they originally intended to hold had they not been hustled out of it as has been described. They also shelled the yeomanry — who were continuing the flank movement — rather heavily as they retired, inflicting some loss.

We had now to wait for the Infantry, and they lagged on the road. The Boer fire began to take effect. Several soldiers were carried wounded off the top of the hill — one poor fellow shot through both cheek-bones. Others had to lie where they were struck because it was not possible to move them while the fire was so accurate.

On the reverse slope, however, there was good cover for man and horse. Some of the men were engaged for the first time, and, though their behaviour was excellent, the General thought it necessary to walk along the firing line and speak a few words here and there.

The infantry still lagged on the road, but at about two o'clock Sir Leslie Rundle himself arrived. The firing about the kopje had been loud, and a rumour — who starts these tales? — ran back along the marching columns that the cavalry were hard pressed, were running short of ammunition, and that the Boers were turning both flanks. At any rate, I found anxious faces in the divisional staff.

Rundle considered that the retention of the kopje was of first importance, and Sir Herbert Chermside, his second in command, fully agreed with him. But the Infantry of the advanced guard were alone near enough. It was decided to push them on. At this moment a reassuring message arrived from Brabazon engaging that he could hold his own, and hoping the Infantry would not be hurried so as to lose their breath.

Everyone was very cheerful after this, and when at last the leading battalion — the Worcester Regiment — marched to the kopje all were able to admire the fine cool way in which they crossed the dangerous ground behind it; and I myself saw three pom-pom shells strike all around a young officer, who waved his rifle thereat in high delight, and shouted out loudly, "By the left!" an order the purport of which I am as uncertain as the reader, but which, doubtless, was encouraging in spirit. When the infantry had relieved the mounted men the latter withdrew to safer positions, and as the evening was drawing on the action came to an end — by mutual consent and by the effective intervention of the British artillery.

The events of the next day, though according to the scale of the war unimportant, were nevertheless instructive from the military point of view, and, so far as they concerned me, sufficiently exciting to require, if not to deserve, a letter to themselves.

CHAPTER FIVE

TWO DAYS WITH BRABAZON (*continued*)

Camp before Dewetsdorp: April 22, 1900

Whether I am to see the white cliffs of Dover again I know not, nor will I attempt to predict. But it seems that my fortunes in this land are to be a succession of adventures and escapes, any one of which would suffice for a personal experience of the campaign. I acquit myself of all desire to seek for these. Indeed, I have zealously tried to avoid all danger except what must attend a War Correspondent's precarious existence. This I recognise as a necessary evil, for the lot of the writer in the field is a hard and heavy one. "All the danger of war and one-half per cent. the glory": such is our motto, and that is the reason why we expect large salaries. But these hazards swoop on me out of a cloudless sky, and that I have hitherto come unscathed through them, while it fills my heart with thankfulness to God for His mercies, makes me wonder why I must be so often thrust to the brink and then withdrawn.

However, I will tell the tale of the doings of the Army, and what happened to me shall fill its proper place, so that the reader may himself be the judge of the matter.

The night of the 20th passed quietly, but the Boers were awake with the sunrise and saluted us with discharges of the pom-pom, which, as far as I could see, did no harm to anyone. We could not press the attack on the previous day because the Infantry were tired out and the enemy's position of sufficient natural strength to make an assault a serious business. In the night the Dutchmen had been busy, and the black lines of entrenchments marked the hillsides. When I inquired whether there would be a battle or not that day, staff officers pointed over he veldt to a column of dust which was coming slowly nearer.

General Campbell, with three battalions (including two of Her Majesty's Guards) and a battery, was marching to join the main column. It was necessary, in view of the entrenchments and the approaching reinforcements, to wait until the force was complete. The event would be decided on the morrow, and meanwhile Brabazon and the mounted troops — cavalry, I shall call them — were to make a reconnaissance of the Boer left.

The brigade, which included the mounted infantry, and was about a thousand strong, moved southward behind the outpost line and, making a rapid and wide circuit, soon came on the enemy's left flank. Here we waited while patrols were pushed out and while Brabazon was cleaning his own right by a still wider turning movement. The patrols soon drew the fire of the Boer pickets, and the rifle shots began to ring out in the clear cool air of the morning. Presently a party of a dozen Boers appeared in the distance, galloping down towards a farm whence they might fire on the gradually advancing cavalry. The General asked the subaltern in charge of our two guns whether they were within range. The young officer was anxious to try. We watched the experiment with attention.

The practice was extremely good. The first shell burst in the middle of the Boer horsemen, who at once spread to a looser formation. The next exploded in front of them, and all the seven shells that were fired fell within measurable distance of someone. For the first time in this war I saw the Boers show what I consider cowardice; for without anyone being killed or wounded the whole party turned back and, abandoning their intention or duty, scurried away to cover behind the long swell of ground over which they had come. The Boer Army in Natal was not thus easily dissuaded from its objects.

Meanwhile the flanking movement was in progress, and as the ground to our right was gradually made good and secure by Colonel Sitwell, Brabazon pushed his centre forward until McNeill's scouts were cantering all over the slopes where the Boers had just been shelled, and hunting such of the enemy as tarried to safer and more remote positions. At last we arrived at the edge of the swell of ground. It fell steeply towards a flat basin, from the middle of which rose a most prominent and peculiar kopje. Invisible behind this was Dewetsdorp. Round it stood Boers, some mounted, some on foot, to the number of about two hundred.

Our rapid advance, almost into the heart of their position, had disturbed and alarmed them. They were doubtful whether this was reconnaissance or actual attack. They determined to make certain by making an attempt to outflank the outflanking Cavalry, and no sooner had our long-range rifle fire compelled them to take cover behind the hill than a new force, as it seemed, of two hundred rode into the open and, passing across our front at a distance of, perhaps, 2,000 yards, made for a white stone kopje on our right.

Angus McNeill ran up to the General: "Sir, may we cut them off? I think we can just do it." The scouts pricked up their ears. The General reflected. "All right," he said, "you may try."

"Mount, mount, mount, the scouts!" cried their impetuous officer, scrambling into his saddle. Then, to me, "Come with us, we'll give you a show now — first-class."

A few days before, in an unguarded moment, I had promised to follow the fortunes of the scouts for a day. I looked at the Boers: they were nearer to the white stone kopje than we, but, on the other hand, they had the hill to climb, and were probably worse mounted. It might be done, and if it were done — I thought of the affair of Action Homes — how dearly they would have to pay in that open plain. So, in the interests of the *Morning Post*, I got on my horse and we all started — forty or fifty scouts, McNeill and I, as fast as we could, by hard spurring, make the horses go.

It was from the very beginning a race, and recognised as such by both sides. As we converged I saw the five leading Boers, better mounted than their comrades, out-pacing the others in a desperate resolve to secure the coign of vantage. I said, "We cannot do it"; but no one would admit defeat or leave the matter undecided. The rest is exceedingly simple.

We arrived at a wire fence 100 yards — to be accurate, 120 yards — from the crest of the kopje, dismounted, and, cutting the wire, were about to seize the precious rock when — as I had seen them in the railway cutting at Frere, grim, hairy, and terrible — the head and shoulders of a dozen Boer appeared; and how many more must be close behind them?

There was a queer, almost inexplicable, pause, or perhaps there was no pause at all; but I seem to remember much happening. First the Boers — one fellow with a long, drooping, black beard, and a chocolate-coloured coat, another with a red scarf round his neck. Two scouts cutting the wire fence stupidly. One man taking aim across his horse, and McNeill's voice, quite steady: "Too late; back to the other kopje. Gallop!"

Then the musketry crashed out, and the "swish" and "whirr" of the bullets filled the air. I put my foot in the stirrup. The horse, terrified at the firing, plunged wildly. I tried to spring into the saddle; it turned under the animal's belly. He broke away, and galloped madly off. Most of the scouts were already 200 yards off. I was alone, dismounted, within the closest range, and a mile at least from cover of any kind.

One consolation I had — my pistol. I could not be hunted down unarmed in the open as I had been before. But a disabling wound was the brightest prospect. I turned, and, for the second time in this war, ran for my life on foot from the Boer marksmen, and I thought to myself, "Here at last I take it." Suddenly, as I ran, I saw a scout. He came from the left, across my front; a tall man, with skull and cross-bones badge, and on a pale horse. Death in Revelation, but life to me.

I shouted to him as he passed: "Give me a stirrup." To my surprise he stopped at once. "Yes," he said shortly. I ran up to him, did not bungle in the business of mounting, and in a moment found myself behind him on the saddle.

Then we rode. I put my arms round him to catch a grip of the man. My hand became soaked with blood. The horse was hard hit; but, gallant beast, he extended himself nobly. The pursuing bullets piped and whistled — for the range was growing longer — overhead.

"Don't be frightened," said my rescuer; "they won't hit you." Then, as I did not reply, "My poor horse, oh my poor — horse; shot with an explosive bullet. The devils! But their hour will come. Oh, my poor horse!"

I said, "Never mind, you've saved my life." "Ah," he rejoined, "but it's the horse I'm thinking about." That was the whole of our conversation.

Judging from the number of bullets I heard I did not expect to be hit after the first 500 yards were covered, for a galloping horse is a difficult target, and the Boers were breathless and excited. But it was with a feeling of relief that I turned the corner of the further kopje and found I had thrown double sixes again.

The result of the race had been watched with strained attention but the rest of the troops, and from their position they knew that we were beaten before we ever reached the wire fence. They had heard the sudden fierce crackle of musketry and had seen what had passed. All the officers were agreed that the man who pulled up in such a situation to help another was worthy of some honourable distinction. Indeed, I have heard that Trooper Roberts — not the name, which seems familiar in this connection — is to have his claims considered for the Victoria Cross. As to this I will not pronounce, for I feel some diffidence in writing impartially of a man who certainly saved me from a great danger.

Well satisfied with my brief experience with the scouts, I returned to General Brabazon. While we had been advancing deeply into the Boer flank, they had not been idle, and now suddenly, from the side of the solitary kopje behind which they had collected, three guns came into action against us. For ten minutes the shell fire was really hot. As these guns were firing with black powder, the smoke springing out in a thick white cloud from the muzzle warned up whenever a projectile was on its way, and, I think, added to the strain on the nerves. You could watch the distant artillery. There was the gun again; four or five seconds to wonder whether the shell would hit you in the face; the approaching hiss rushing into a rending shriek; safe over; bang! right among the horses a hundred yards behind. Here comes the next — two guns fired together this time. Altogether, the Boers fired nearly thirty shells — several of which were shrapnel — on this small space of ground. But fate was in a merciful mood that day, for we had but one man killed and five or six — including the General's orderly — wounded by them.

It was, however, evident that this could not endure. Brabazon had not cared to bring his own two guns into such an advanced position, because they were not horse guns, and might not be able to get away safely if the Boers should make a strong counter-attack. Indeed, so long as the loss of guns is considered a national disaster instead of only an ordinary incident of war, cavalry officers will regard them rather as sources of anxiety than as powerful weapons.

Without guns it was useless to stay, and as, moreover, Sir Leslie Rundle's orders were that the cavalry were not to be severely engaged, Brabazon decided to withdraw the reconnaissance, and did so most successfully, after an instructive little rearguard action. He had penetrated far into the enemy's position; had compelled him to move his guns and disturb his frontal dispositions; had reconnoitered the ground, located the laagers, and come safely away with the loss of little more than a dozen men. Had there been on this day an infantry support behind the cavalry we should have hustled the enemy out of his whole position and slept triumphantly in Dewetsdorp.

Sir Leslie Rundle was much impressed by the vigor and success of the cavalry, whose fortunes were watched from the plateau, and as evening came the report spread through the camp that a general engagement would be fought on the next day. He also decided to entrust the direction of the actual turning attack to General Brabazon, who, besides his cavalry force, was to have twelve guns and an infantry brigade under his command.

With every feeling of confidence in the issue the army went to bed, impatient for the dawn. But in the dead of night a telegram arrived from Lord Roberts, instructing Rundle not to press his attack until he was in touch with Pole-Carew and other reinforcements; and it thus became evident that he operations had grown to an altogether larger scale.

CHAPTER SIX

THE DEWETSDORP EPISODE

Bloemfontein: May 1, 1900

Sometimes it happens that these letters are devoted to describing small incidents, and often personal experiences, in a degree of detail which, if the rest of the campaign were equally narrated, would expand the account to limits far beyond the industry of the writer or the patience of the reader. At others many important events must be crowded into a few pages. But though the proportions of the tale may vary, I shall not deserve criticism so long as the original object of conveying a lively impression of the war is strictly pursued; nor should the reader complain if, for his instruction or amusement, he is made one day to sit with the map of the Orange Free State spread before him, and move little flags to show the course of the operations, and on another day is invited to share the perils of a scout's patrol or try the chances of a cavalry skirmish. To-day there is much to tell, and we must remain almost beyond the sound of the cannon watching a distance panorama.

The object of the operations was in any case to relieve Wepener, and to clear the right-hand bottom corner of the Orange Free State of the Boers, and, if the enterprise prospered and the fates were kind, to cut off and capture some part of their forces. In all five columns were in motion. There were to be demonstrations along the east of the railway line, increasing in earnestness according as they were nearer the south, and the lowest columns were to actually push the matter through. Ian Hamilton, with 2,000 mounted infantry, was ordered to demonstrate against the waterworks position. French, supported by Pole-Carew, was instructed to move on Leeukop. Rundle, in conjunction with Hart and Brabant from the southward, was to force his way to Dewetsdorp and to relieve Wepener. What befell his column on April 20 and 21 has already been described. The attack on the Boer position in front of Dewetsdorp had not been made on the 20th because Sir Herbert Chermside pointed out that the infantry was fatigued with marching. The next morning the smooth hills were crowed with entrenchments, and it was thought better to wait for Campbell's Brigade, which would arrive at sundown.

The 22nd was to be the day of battle. Meanwhile Sir Leslie Rundle had telegraphed to Lord Roberts describing the horseshoe position of the enemy, and its strength, explaining that with the small mounted force at his disposal any attack which he might make would develop into something very like a frontal attack, and would be costly. A strong memorandum had previously been circulated among divisional and brigade commanders condemning, almost prohibiting, frontal attacks, and the General, not unnaturally, wished to assure himself that the price of victory would not be grudged. When this telegram reached Bloemfontein it was apparently misunderstood. "Rundle is hung up," they said. "He can't get on"; and hence the reply which arrived in the dead of night and prevented the attack of the 22nd. "Wait till you get in touch with Pole-Carew," or words to that effect. So the powerful force — almost equal in strength to that with which Sir George White had resisted the first fury of the Boers when, with 25,000 men under the Commandant-General himself, they burst into Natal — was relegated to some days of pusillanimous waiting in front of a position held by scarcely 2.500 men.

After breakfast on the morning of the unfought battle I climbed to the top of the hill the cavalry had seized two days before, and which the soldiers had christened "Brab's kopje". A fifteen hundred yards musketry duel was proceeding, and it was dangerous to put one's head over the stone shelters even for a minute to look at the Boer entrenchments on the green slope opposite. But such was not my purpose. I scanned the northern horizon. It was Pole-Carew. Half an hour later another star began to twinkle further to the eastward. French and his cavalry were riding steadily forward, "fighting, too," said the heliographs, "but pushing them back". The scale of the operations had grown indeed. No less than five infantry and three cavalry brigades, with more than seventy guns, were involved in the business of dislodging 2,500 Boer from their position in front of Dewetsdorp.

The 23rd passed quietly, except for an intermittent bombardment of our camp by the Dutch guns and Vickers-Maxim and the usual patter of musketry along the outposts. The diamond points on the distant hills seemed nearer and more to the east than before, and in the afternoon Brabazon was sent to reconnoitre towards them. As the yeomanry emerged from the shelter of the plateau the Boer Creusot gun espied them. Brabazon, with half a dozen officers or orderlies, was riding fifty yards in front of his brigade.

"See there," said the Dutch gunner, "there is the Hoofd Commandant himself; take good aim." So they did, and from a range of 5,000 yards burst their shell within two yards of the General's horse. "Wonderful," said Brabazon; "why can't our forsaken artillery shoot like that?" and he ordered the brigade to canter by troops across the dangerous ground. I watched the scene that followed from comparative safety, 600 yards nearer the Boer gun. Troop by troop the yeomanry emerged from shelter. As each did so the men opened out to dispersed order and began to gallop; and for every troop there was one shell. Between the shrieking of the shell overhead and its explosion among the galloping horsemen there was an appreciable interval, in which one might easily have wagered whether it would hit or miss.

The yeomanry were very steady, and for the most part ran the gauntlet at a nice, dignified canter, pulling into a walk as soon as the dangerous space was crossed. After all no one was hurt, except three men who broke their crowns through their horses falling on the rocky ground. Indeed, I think, speaking from some experience, that we can always treat these Creusot 9-pounders with contempt. They fling a small shell an immense distance with surprising accuracy, but unless they actually hit someone they hardly every do any harm. An ordinary bullet is just as dangerous, though it does not make so much noise.

At Vaal Krantz, in Natal, Dundonald's Brigade and other troops lived quite comfortably for three days under the fire of a 98-pounder gun, which in all that time only killed one solider of the Dublin Fusiliers, two natives, and a few beasts. The wholesale aspect of artillery fire is not obtained unless at least a dozen guns are firing percussion shell or unless shrapnel can be used. At present the Boers often cause us a great deal of trouble with single guns, which, though they do scarcely any material harm, disturb everyone, so that camps are shifted and marching columns ordered to make long *détours*; whereas we ought to shrug our shoulders, as Ladysmith did, pay the small necessary toll, and go our ways uninterruptedly. But I am being drawn into detail and discussion, which, if I am ever to catch up the swift march of events, must be rigorously excluded.

The 23rd passed quietly for times of war, and the Boer riflemen and artillerists fired busily till dusk without doing much harm. We wondered how much they knew of the "increased scale" of the operations. Did they realise the enormous strength of the forces closing round them? It was hardly likely. Yet they were certainly holding all their positions in force at nightfall, and meanwhile the spring of the trap was compressed, and the moment for releasing it arrived.

The morning of the 24th was unbroken by a single shot. Rundle, now in touch with Pole-Carew, swung his division to the left, pivoting on Chermside, to whom he entrusted the defence of the plateau. Brabazon with his Mounted Brigade formed the extreme outer flank of this sweeping movement. His orders were to join French, who drove inward from the north, somewhere behind Dewetsdorp on the Modder River. So we started, and, with much caution and the pomp of war, turned the enemy's left, and in solemn silence bore down on the flank and rear of his position.

Meanwhile, Chermside on the plateau was struck by the entire cessation of fire from the Boer lines opposite to him. He sent scouts to reconnoitre. Single men crept up the hill, looked into the trenches, and found — nothing. The Boers had retreated swiftly in the night. They enjoyed good information of all our movements and designs: had foreseen the impossibility of withstanding the great forces operating against them. They delayed us with the appearance of strength until the last minute. On the night of the 22nd they sent off their waggons towards Thabanchu. On the 23rd they made their effort against Wepener, and attacked the garrison heavily, and on the night of the 24th, having failed at Wepener, they performed a masterly retreat, the assailants of Wepener marching northwards *via* Ladybrand, the covering force at Dewetsdorp moving toward Thabanchu.

And so it was that when, as directed, Brabazon circled round the enemy's left flank and struck the Modder River — here only a rocky ditch with occasional pools of mud — and when French, moving from Leeukop round and behind their right flank, met him, they found the Dutch already departed, and Dewetsdorp again under the Union Jack. The strong jaws of the rat-trap shut together with a snap. I saw them — back across the open plain — two great horns of cavalry and guns; but the rat had walked comfortably away some hours before. Chermside moving over the empty trenches occupied the town. Rundle, reaching it an hour later, owing to his turning movement, hurried on through it to the Modder, and laid Brabazon's dusty squadrons on the retreating enemy. Indeed, the latter officer was already at the trot towards Thabanchu when French himself arrived — a large and magnificent staff, "pom-poms", horse artillery, and two cavalry brigades — and assumed supreme command.

He immediately stopped the pursuit, sent Brabazon back to relieve Wepener — which place had by its plucky defence, like Jellalabad, relieved itself — and entered Dewetsdorp, where he remained until the next day.

Such is the story of Dewetsdorp, which cannot be contemplated with feelings of wild enthusiasm. The Wepener situation was cleared up, and the Boers were persuaded to retire from the right-hand bottom corner of the Free State towards Ladybrand and Thabanchu at an exceedingly small price in blood. On the other hand, the enemy might boast that 2,500 burghers with six runs had contained 13,000 troops with thirty guns for a week, while their brethren worked their wicked will on Wepener, and had only been dislodged by the setting in motion of more than 25,000 men and seventy guns.

The movement which followed the occupation of Dewetsdorp need not take long in the telling. French's occupation of the town instead of pursuing the enemy was not in accordance with the Commander-in-Chief's ideas, and the cavalry leader was forthwith ordered to follow the Boers at his best pace to Thabanchu. He started accordingly at daylight on the 25th, and Rundle with the Eighth Division followed at noon. Chermside remained at Dewets-dorp with part of the Third Division, and was entrusted with the re-establishment of order through the disturbed districts.

Brabazon marched on Wepener and collected the garrison. Their defence of seventeen days, under continual rifle and shell fire, in hastily dug trenches, which they were unable to leave even at night; exposed to several fierce attacks; in spite of heavy losses and with uncertain prospects of relief, will deserve careful attention when full accounts are published, and is a very honourable episode in the history of Brabant's Colonial Brigade, and particularly in the records of the Cape Mounted Rifles, who lost nearly a quarter of their strength.

Bringing the defenders with him, and having communicated with Hart and Brabant, Brabazon returned to Dewetsdorp, and was ordered to move thence to Thabanchu, which he did in an exceed-ingly convenient hour, as it turned out, for a certain convoy with an escort of Scots Guards and yeomanry. Pole-Carew and the Eleventh Division returned to Bloemfontein to take part in the main advance.

The Boers made good their retreat. They took with them twenty-five prisoners of the Worcester Regiment, who had blun-dered into their camp before Dewetsdorp, armed only with cooking pots, which they meant to carry to their regiment on "Brab's kopje", and great quantities of sheep and oxen. They halted in Ladybrand, and to the north and east of Thabanchu, in a most pugnacious mood. Indeed, they had no reason to be discontented with the result of their southern incursion.

They had captured seven guns and nearly 1,000 prisoners. They had arrested and carried off a good many farmers who had laid down their arms and made their peace with the British Government. They had harried all who received the troops kindly, had collected large quantities of supplies, which they had sent north, and, lastly, had delayed the main advance by more than five weeks.

Owing to the great disproportion of the forces, the fighting had not been of a severe nature, and the losses were small. In the skirmishes before Dewetsdorp, about forty men were killed and wounded, mostly in Brabazon's Brigade. In the action at Leeukop and the subsequent fighting which attended French's march several officers and fifty men were stricken, and a squadron of the 9th Lancers, which was required to attack a kopje, suffered severely, having nearly twenty casualties, including Captain Stanley, a very brave officer, who died of his wounds, and Victor Brooke (of whom more will be heard in the future) who had his left hand smashed. Captain Brazier-Creagh, 9th Bengal Lancers, commanding Robert's Horse, was killed at Leeukop, and his many friends along the Indian frontier will not need to be told that by his death Lord Robert's Army suffered a loss appreciable even among the great forces now in the field.

CHAPTER SEVEN

IAN HAMILTON'S MARCH

Winburg: May 8, 1900

The unsatisfactory course of the operations in the south-eastern corner of the Free State, and the indecisive results to which they led, were soon to be arrested and reversed by a series of movements of surprising vigour and remarkable success. Of all the demonstrations which had been intended against the enemy to the east of the railway, Hamilton's advance towards the waterworks position, being the most northerly, was to have been the least earnestly pressed. The orders were: "If you find the waterworks weakly held, which is not likely, you may try to occupy them, and, in the event of success, may call up Smith-Dorrien's Brigade to strengthen you."

On this, General Ian Hamilton, who now commanded the imposing, but somewhat scattered, Mounted Infantry Division, started from Bloemfontein on the 22nd of April with about 2,000 Light Horse, Australians, and mounted infantry, and one battery of Horse Artillery.

On the 23rd he arrived before the waterworks, reconnoitred them, found them weakly held, or, at any rate, thought he could take them, attacked, and before dark made himself master of the waterworks themselves, and of the drift over the river which led to the hills beyond, into which the enemy had retired. Smith-Dorrien's Brigade was called up at once, arrived after dark, and the next morning the forces crossed at the drift, and the whole position was occupied. The enemy offered a slight resistance, which was attributed by some to a deep design on their part to lure the column into a trap further to the east, and by others to the manner in which the attack was delivered. The news of the capture of this strong and important place, which secures the Bloemfontein water supply, was received with great satisfaction at headquarters.

Meanwhile the operations round Dewetsdorp came to their abortive conclusion, and it became evident that the Boers had evaded the intercepting columns and were making their way northwards by Thabanchu. What was to be done? Had the officer commanding the waterworks any suggestion to make? Most certainly, and the suggestion was that he should be permitted to advance himself and occupy Thabanchu. This was the answer that was expected and desired. Permission, and with it a field battery, was accordingly given, and, on the 25th of April, the column moved out of the water-works position towards Thabanchu. It consisted of Ridley's Brigade of Mounted Infantry, which included a large proportion of colonials — Australians and New Zealanders — Smith-Dorrien's Infantry Brigade (Gordons, Canadians, Shropshires, and Cornwalls), with twelve guns.

The country to the east of Bloemfontein is at first smooth and open. Great plains of brownish grass stretch almost to the horizon, broken to the eye only by occasional scrub-covered hills. To anyone unaccustomed to the South African veldt they appear to offer no obstacle to the free movement of cavalry or artillery; nor is it until one tries to ride in a straight line across them that the treacherous and unimagined donga or the awkward wire fence interposes itself. But beyond the Modder River, on which the waterworks are situated, the surface of the ground becomes rocky and hilly, and the features increase in prominence until Thabanchu Mountain is reached, and thereafter the country uprears itself in a succession of ridges to the rugged and lofty peaks of Basutoland.

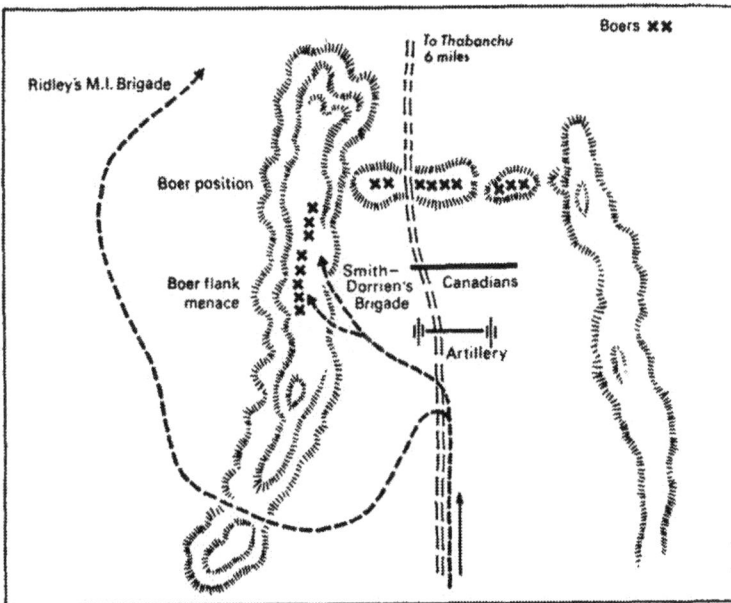

DIAGRAM EXPLAINING HAMILTON'S ACTION AT ISRAEL'S POORTE, THE 25TH OF APRIL

Thabanchu, a small village, as we should regard it in England, a town of comparative commercial importance in the Orange Free State, and of undoubted strategic value during this phase of the operations, stands at the foot of the precipitous feature that bears its name. It is approached from the direction of Bloemfontein by a long, broad, flat-bottomed valley, whose walls on either side rise higher and higher by degrees as the road runs eastward. The eastern end of this wide passage is closed by a chain of rocky kopjes, whose situation is so curious and striking that they seem to be devised by nature to resist the advance of an invader. The kopjes, rising abruptly from the flat glacis-like ground, are a strong rampart, and the whole position, resting on apparently secure flanks, creates a most formidable barrier, which is called locally Israel's Poorte.

Along the valley, on the 25th of April, Hamilton proceeded to march with his entire force, Ridley and the mounted infantry being a considerable distance in front of the main body. At ten o'clock a heavy fire of musketry and artillery was opened at an extreme range from the hills on the left-hand side of the column. Ignoring this, which proved afterwards to be only a Boer demonstration, Ridley continued his march, and Hamilton followed, until, at a little after eleven o'clock, both were brought to a standstill before the Israel's Poorte position, which was found to be occupied by the enemy, estimated at 800 strong, with several guns.

After a personal reconnaissance, and in spite of a most disquieting report that the Boers had just been reinforced by "two thousand men in four lines", the General resolved to attack. His plan was simple but effective. It resembled very closely Sir Bindon Blood's forcing of the "Gate of Swat" at Landakai in 1897. The front was to be masked and contained by a sufficient force of Infantry and all the guns. The rest of the troops were to stretch out to the left and swing to the right, the infantry along the left-hand wall of the valley, the mounted men actually the other side of the wall.

Accordingly, the Canadian Regiment and the Grahamstown Volunteers (Marshall's House) moved forward in extended order — 25 yards interval between men — to within about 800 yards of the enemy's position and here, just out of the range of serious harm, they lay down and opened a continuous musketry fire. Both batteries came into action forthwith and shelled the crest line with satisfactory energy. Smith-Dorrien, with the remaining three battalions of his brigade, moved to the left, and began working along the ridges, Ridley, breaking out of the valley into the more open ground beyond, began to move against the enemy's line of retreat.

Four hours passed, during which the Boers indulged the hope that the frontal attack would be pushed home, and at the end of which they found their right flank turned and their rear threatened. Immediately, with all the hurry of undisciplined troops who feel a hand on their communications, they evacuated the position, and, running to their horses, galloped away. The Canadians and Grahamstown Volunteers thereupon arose and occupied the line of kopjes, and thus the door was opened and the road to Thabanchu cleared. Our losses in this smart action were about twenty killed and wounded, among whom were no less than five officers of the Grahamstown Volunteers. The Dutch left five corpses on the field, and doubtless carried away a score of wounded.

General Hamilton, pushing on, entered Thabanchu the same night, and the British flag was again hoisted over the town. The Imperialist section of the community, who had in the interval between the evacuation and reoccupation of the town been subjected to much annoyance at the hands of the Boers, were naturally shy, and afraid to make any sign of welcome. The southern commandos whom Dewetsdorp and Wepener had, by hard marching already passed behind Thabanchu with their convoys. On the 26th French and his cavalry, covering the march of Rundle's (Eighth) Division, arrived, and, since he was a lieutenant-general, took the command out of Hamilton's hands for a time.

I had come northwards from Dewetsdorp with the cavalry brigades, and was an eye-witness of the operations round Thabanchu which occupied the 26th and 27th. Thabanchu Mountain is a lofty and precipitous feature of considerable extent, and, towards the south, of indefinite shape. To the north, however, it presents a wide bay, on whose grassy shores rising from the more arid plain the Boer laagers were reported to stand. The enemy held the crest of the crescent-shaped mountain with guns and riflemen, and in order that no one should pry behind it they extended on their right a few hundred trustworthy fellows, who, working in the most scattered formation, gave to their position an enormous front of doubtful strength.

On the afternoon of the 26th, with a view to further operations on the following day, a force of mounted infantry, supported by galloping Maxims and a horse battery, was sent to reconnoitre, and if possible to hold the hill, henceforward called "Kitchener's Horse Hill". The troops gained possession of the feature without fighting, though a few Boers were seen galloping along the ridges to the right and left, and an intermittent musketry fire began. A garrison to hold the hill was detailed, consisting of Kitchener's Horse, a company of the Lincoln Mounted Infantry, and two Maxim guns; but just as the sun sank this plan was changed by the officer commanding the force, and the whole were ordered to retire into Thabanchu. On the Indian frontier it is a cardinal rule to retire by daylight and sit still when overtaken by night in the best position at hand. In this war experience has shown that it is usually better to remain on the ground, even at a heavy cost, until it is quite dark, and then to retreat, if necessary. The reason of the difference is that while close contact with an Afridi armed with a four-foot knife, active as a cat and fierce as a tiger, is to be avoided as much as possible, no soldier asks better than the closest contact with a Dutchman. But though the teaching of both wars may seem contradictory on many points, on one point it is in complete agreement: twilight is the worst time of all to retire.

The consequences of this ill-timed change of plan were swift. The Boers saw the retrograde movement, and pressed boldly forward, and Kitchener's Horse, finding themselves closely engaged, were unable to move. A sharp and savage little fight followed in the gloom. The Boers crept quite close to the soldiers, and one fierce greybeard was shot through the head eight paces from the British firing line, but not until after he had killed his man. The reports which reached the town, that Kitchener's Horse were "cut off" on a kopje four miles from the camp, induced General French to send the Gordon Highlanders to their relief. This battalion started at about ten o'clock, and were put on their road to the northward. But in the darkness and the broken ground they lost their way, marched five miles to the south, occupied another hill, and did not rejoin the command until the afternoon of the next day, an absence which, since no inquires could discover them, caused much anxiety. Kitchener's Horse meanwhile, under Major Fowle, of the 21st Lancers, made a plucky defence, beat off the Boers, and managed at about eleven o'clock to effect their retreat undisturbed. The losses in the affair where twelve to fourteen men killed and wounded, including one officer, who was shot through the head.

Very early the next morning the whole force marched out of the town, and French's operations were this day designed to compel the enemy to retreat from his positions in rear of Thabanchu Mountain, and if possible to surround some part of his force. The information at General French's disposal could not, however, have been very accurate, for in my telegram of the 26th I wrote that "more than 2,000 Boers" were collected to the north of Thabanchu, and the Press Censor erased this and substituted the words "small parties". If this latter view had been correct it is probable that the operations of the following day would have been attended by a greater measure of success.

The plan was clear and vigorous. Gordon's Cavalry Brigade was to move to the right, round the east of Thabanchu Mountain, and force their way into the plains behind it. It was hoped that the Lancers, of which this brigade is entirely composed, would find some opportunity for using their dreaded weapon. Hamilton was to push back the weak Boer right, and open the way for Dickson's Cavalry Brigade to pass through and join hands with Gordon. Rundle, whose infantry were tired from their long march from Dewetsdorp, was to demonstrate against the Boers' centre and hold the town.

The action opened with the re-occupation of Kitchener's Horse Hill by Smith-Dorrien's Infantry Brigade, who advanced in determined style, and by a sweeping movement of Ridley's Mounted Infantry. Both these undertakings, which were directed by Hamilton, prospered. The Boer right, which was very thin, was brushed aside, and the road for the Cavalry was opened. At, and not until, nine o'clock, French's leading squadrons began to appear on the plain, and by ten the whole of Dickson's Brigade had passed through the gap and were safely extended in the undulating plains beyond.

Wishing to see, for the first time, cavalry and horse artillery working in suitable country, I rode down from my post of observation on Kitchener's Horse Hill and trotted and cantered until I caught up the squadrons. It was evident that the left enveloping arm was making good progress. Already we could almost look into the bay behind Thabanchu Mountain. If Gordon were only getting on as well we might join hands with him, and enclasp a goodly catch of prisoners. So the brigade continued to advance from ridge to ridge, and presently Boers began to gallop across the front to escape, as was thought, from the net we were drawing round them. At all of these the horse artillery and the pom-poms — British pom-poms at last — fired industriously. But as the enemy kept a respectful distance and an open formation, only a few were seen to fall. The others did not fly very far, but gathered together in what soon became considerable numbers outside the net, near a peaked hill, which does not appear in my sketch, but which the reader may bear in mind as lying to the left rear of the turning cavalry.

At last Dickson's advance reached a point between Thabanchu Mountain and the peaked hill, so that no more Boers could escape by that road; and we saw the others, three or four hundred in number, riding about, up and down, or round and round in the bay, like newly-caught rats in a cage.

At this everyone became very excited. "Gordon must have headed them back," it was said. "Only a few more men and we might make a bag." Where could men be found? Somebody suggested asking Hamilton. The helio twinkled: "Come and help us make a bag", it said, in somewhat more formal language. And Hamilton came forthwith, leaving positions which were of much value; collecting every man he could lay his hands on — weary mounted infantry, a tired-out battery, and all of Smith-Dorrien's Brigade that could march fast at the end of a long day — he hurried to seize and line the northern spurs of Thabanchu Mountain, prepared to risk much to strike a heavy blow.

The movement of infantry and guns to support him encouraged Dickson to press still further forward, and the whole brigade advanced nearly another mile. At length we overtopped a smooth ridge, and found ourselves looking right into the bay or horseshoe of mountains. Now at last we must see Gordon. "There he is," cried

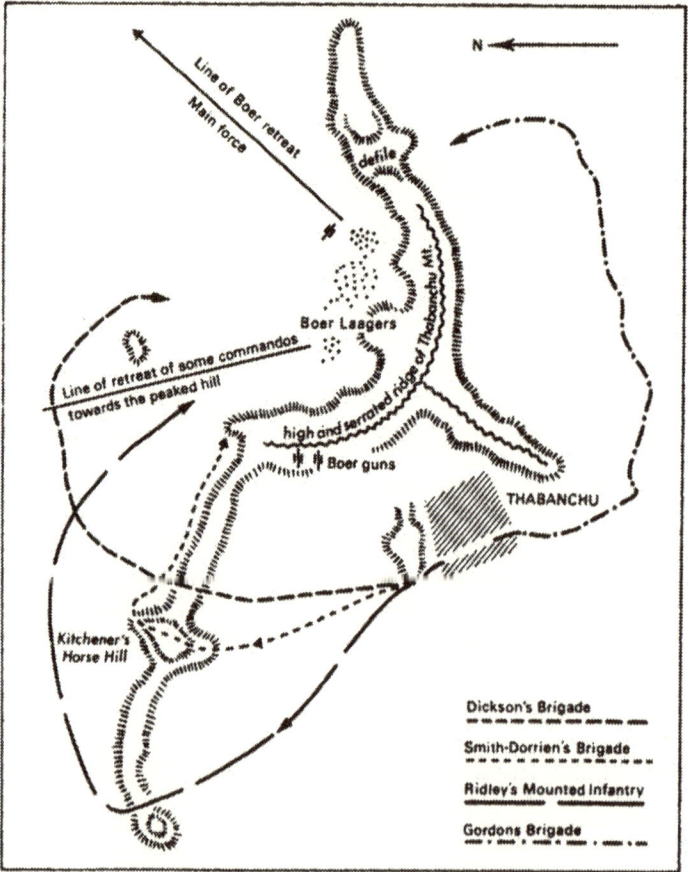

DIAGRAM EXPLAINING FRENCH'S OPERATIONS ROUND
THABANCHU, THE 26TH AND 27TH APRIL

several voices, and looking in the direction shown I saw a majestic body of horse streaming out of the centre of the bay towards the north-west. But was it Gordon? At least 4,000 mounted men were riding across our front, hardly two miles away. Surely no brigade was no numerous. Yet such was the precision of the array that I could not believe them Boers.

Boers their numbers, however, proved them to be; and not their numbers alone, for before we had watched this striking spectacle long, two large puffs of smoke leaped from the tail of the hostile column, and two well-aimed shells burst near our horse battery. At the same time patrols from the left rear hurried in with the news that the Boers who had already escaped from our imagined "trap" were advancing in force, with two more guns, to cut us from the rest of the army.

As for Gordon, there was no longer any doubt about his fortunes. Far away to the eastward the horseshoe wall of mountains dipped to a pass, and on the sides of this gateway little puffs of smoke, dirty brown against the darkening sky, showed that Gordon was still knocking with his artillery at the door, and had never been able to debouch in the plains behind it. Moreover, the dangerous hour of twilight was not long distant. Dickson determined to retreat while time remained, and did so without any unnecessary delay. Whereat the Boers came down on our rear and flank, opening furious fire at long range, and galloping eagerly forward, so that the brigade and its guns, so far from entrapping the enemy, were all but entrapped themselves; indeed, the brigadier's mess cart, the regimental water carts, and several other little things, which, being able only to trot, could not "conform to the general movement", were snapped up by the hungry enemy, who now pressed on exulting.

Meanwhile Hamilton had taken some risks in order to promote the expected entrapping. He had now to think for himself. First, the Boer advance must be stopped, and, secondly, the force which had, in the hopes of grasping the Boers, let go its hold on Kitchener's Horse Hill, must be withdrawn within the Thabanchu picket line. The General, however, was equal to both requirements. Judiciously arranging some force of infantry and gun, he peppered the advancing Boers heavily, so that at 800 yards they wheeled about and scurried to the shelter of adjacent kopjes. This advantage restored the situation. Hamilton regained the ground till dark, and then, with the whole of Ridley's and Smith-Dorrien's commands, returned safely into Thabanchu.

During the day rifle and artillery fire had been constant; but as the fighting had been conducted at extreme ranges, which neither side showed much anxiety to diminish, the slaughter was small. Indeed, I do not think that a dozen men were stricken in either army. So far as the British were concerned, the result of the day's operations was a qualified success.

The Boers were evidently prepared to retreat from Thabanchu, but they proposed to do so in their own time and at their most excellent discretion, and it was quite evident that we had not succeeded in any way in hindering or preventing them. It was also clear that, far from being "in small parties", their strength was nearly 6,000, so that on the whole we might congratulate ourselves on having moved in ignorance and taken no great hurt. The only point about the action difficult to understand was the behaviour of the Boers who had ridden about like caged rats. Why should they do so when they knew that their line of retreat to the north-east was perfectly secure? I can only conclude that this particular commando had arranged to retire northwards towards the peaked hill, and were annoyed at being prevented from joining their comrades at the point where their waggons, and, consequently, their dinners, were awaiting them.

On the evening of this instructive, but unsatisfactory, day, Hamilton received orders from Lord Roberts to march north on Winburg to conformity with the general advance of the army. For this purpose his force was to be largely increased, and the operations which followed require the space of another letter. French remained for some days at Thabanchu, but attempted no further serious operations against the enemy.

Only one other incident of interest occurred in the neighbourhood of Thabanchu. After his relief of Wepener, Brabazon was ordered thither *via* Dewetsdorp. On the 28th, dusty and tired at the end of a long march, he arrived with his Yeomanry at the foot of a pass among the hills. A Kaffir lounged into the bivouac and asked the General whether he would like to see some pretty shelling, for that there was a fine show at the top of the valley. Brabazon, much interested, mounted his horse forthwith, and, guided by the Kaffir through devious paths, reached a point which afforded an extensive view.

There, in the twilight, lay a British convoy, stoutly defended by a company of the kiddies and a few yeomanry, and shelled — as the Kaffir had said — with great precision by two Boer guns. The General thereupon gave the Kaffir a "fiver" to carry a letter through the Boer lines to the commander of the convoy, telling that officer to hold out manfully, and promising that with the dawn Brabazon and the Imperial Yeomanry would come to his aid.

The Kaffir succeeded in his mission. The convoy was encouraged, and, good as his word, with the daylight came the General, at whose approach the Boers fled incontinently, so that Brabazon, the yeomanry, and the convoy came in safely and triumph into Thabanchu together.

CHAPTER EIGHT

IAN HAMILTON

London: August 10, 1900

Ian Standish Monteith Hamilton was born at Corfu in 1853. His father, the late Colonel Christian Monteith Hamilton — then a captain, but who eventually commanded the 92nd Highlanders — was the eldest son of John George Hamilton and of Christina Cameron Monteith, daughter of Henry Monteith of Carstairs, sometime Member of Parliament for Lanarkshire. His mother, the later Maria Corinna Vereker, was the daughter of John, third Viscount Gort, by Maria O'Grady, daughter of Viscount Guillamore.[1] The Hamilton family is one of the elder branches of the Scottish Hamiltons, and represents the male line of the Hamiltons of Westport. One of his ancestors on his father's side, a Colonel Hamilton, was for several years an aide-de-camp of the first Duke of Marlborough, and it was therefor something in the nature of a coincidence when Ian Hamilton found the present Duke of Marlborough serving in a similar capacity on his staff. It would not be quite correct to call him a pure Celt, but some notice should be taken by those interested in these questions that his blood is mostly Celtic stock, Scottish and Irish respectively.

When Ian Hamilton was born his father was serving with a detachment of the 92nd Highlanders at Corfu. His mother died in 1856, and for the next ten years, the father being constantly on duty with the regiment, he and his younger brother, Vereker Hamilton, who was born in 1856, lived with their grandparent at Hapton, in the Holy Loch in Argyllshire. Such a childhood on moor and loch in a fine wild country was likely to develop and brace nerve and muscle, and stir the keep blood inherited from many generations of warlike ancestors. He was educated first at Cheam, and as he grew sufficiently old, at Wellington College. Here he was very happy, and although he was not especially noted for industry, his success in the examinations at the end of each tern excused any neglect in its course. In 1872 he passed the tests for the army, and, according to the system at that time in force, was offered the choice of going to

1 *Vide* Peerage, Gort and Guillamore.

Sandhurst or living for a year abroad to learn a foreign language thoroughly. The cadet chose the latter, and was sent to Germany. Here he had the good luck to make the close friendship of a most distinguished old man. General Dammers was a Hanoverian who had fought against the Prussians at Langezalze, and who, refusing a very high command under the Prussians, lived at Dresden. Although he himself remained the aide-de-camp to the ex-King of Hanover, he became the centre of a group of Hanoverian officers who had entered the Saxon service. He was thus in touch with the latest school of military thought, stimulated to its utmost activity by the lessons of the great war which had lately been concluded. From General Dammers, Ian Hamilton learned the German language, military surveying, something of military history, and something doubtless of strategy and the art of war. The year thus passed very profitably. On his return to England, however, the War Office announced that they had changed their minds and that for the future everybody must go through Sandhurst. Such protests as his father, himself an officer, was entitled to make were overruled by the authorities, and Ian Hamilton embarked upon his military career having lost, through no fault of his own, one year of seniority — a year which Fortune had perhaps even then determined to restore to him manifold.

In 1873 he entered the 12th Foot, and after some months joined his father's old regiment, the 92nd. At first with the 92nd, and after 1881 with the 2nd battalion of the regiment, the Gordon Highlander, Ian Hamilton followed the drum from garrison to garrison, going through the military routine, and plodding slowly up the first few steps of the long ladder of promotion. From the very first he interested himself in musketry. He became himself a keen and good rifle shot, and not with the military rifle alone. He spent a long leave in Kashmir on the fringe of the snows, and made a remarkable bag. Indeed, some of his heads attained nearly to the record dimensions, and one big single-horned markhor enjoyed the actual supremacy for several months.

Then came the Afghan war. Ian Hamilton, although only an infantry soldier, became aide-de-camp, with Brabazon as Brigade Major. Early in the campaign he was stricken down with fever, and so avoided being drawn into the controversy which raged for several years in military circles around the action in the Chardeh valley. It would indeed have been unfortunate if at this early stage in his career he had been led into any antagonism to the great General with whom his fortunes were afterwards so closely associated.

The Boer war of 1881 found Hamilton still a subaltern. He was ordered to South Africa with his regiment, and went full of eager anticipation. The regiment, composed almost entirely of soldiers inured to the hardships and disdainful of the dangers of war, was in the most perfect condition to encounter the enemy, and, as is usual in British expeditions on the outward voyage, they despised him most thoroughly. It was not to be dreamed of that a parcel of ragged Boers should stand against the famous soldiers of Kabul and Kandahar. They discussed beforehand the clasps which would be given upon the metal for the campaign. They were to be Laing's Nek, Relief of Potchefstroom, and Pretoria 1881. No one had then ever heard the name of Majuba Mountain. Yet there was to be the first encounter between Highlanders and Dutchmen.

The dismal story of Majuba is better known than its importance deserves. Had that action been fought in this war it would perhaps have gone down to history as the affair of the 27th of February. Instead, it was accepted as a stricken field, and might, such was the significance that was attached to it, have changed the history of nations. It needs no repetition here save in so far as it is concerned with Ian Hamilton. Majuba Mountain may be general terms be described as a saucer-topped hill. Sir George Colley and his six hundred soldiers, picked from various units (that all might share the glory), sat themselves down to rest and sleep, and dig a well in the bottom of the saucer. One weak picket of Gordon Highlanders was thrust forward over the rim on to the outer slope of the hill to keep an eye on those silent grey patches which marked the Boer laagers far below. Hamilton was the subaltern in command. As the day gradually broke and the light grew stronger, he saw from the very lifting of the curtain the course of the tragedy. Boers awoke, bustled about their encampments; looked up just as Symons's Brigade looked up on the morning of Talana Hill, and saw the skyline fringed with men. More bustle, long delay, much argument and hesitation below, a little boooting rifle fire from some of the British soldiers: "Ha, ha! got you this time I think!" — and then, straggle of horsemen riding in tens and twenties towards the foot of the mountain. Hamilton reported accordingly. The action of Majuba Hill had begun. Pause.

There was — so it has been described to me — a long donga that led up the steep slope. Into the lower end of this the Boer horsemen disappeared. Hamilton moved his score of men a little to their right, where they might command this zig-zag approach as much as the broken ground would allow, and reported again to the General or whoever was directing affairs — for Colley, wearied with the tremendous exertion of the night climb, was sleeping — "Enemy advancing to attack." He also made a few stone shelters. Pause again. Suddenly, quite close, darting forward here and there among the rocks and bushes of the donga — Boers! Fire on them, then. The Gordons' rifles spluttered accordingly, and back came the answer hot and sharp — a close and accurate musketry fire pinning the little party of Regulars to the earth behind their flimsy shelters. No one could show his head to fire. Soldiers would hold a helmet up above the sheltering stone and bring it down with two and three bullets through it. Could half a company fight a battle by itself? What were others doing? Hamilton felt bound to send another report. He left the half company in charge of the sergeant, got up, ran up the slope, and dropped into safety the other side of the saucer-shaped rim. The distance was scarcely forty yards, yet two bullets passed through his kilt in crossing it. Where was the General? A staff officer, ignorant and therefore undisturbed, said that the General was sleeping. "He knew," said the staff officer, "what was going on. No need for a subaltern of Highlanders to concern himself." Hamilton returned, running the gauntlet again, to his men. The fire grew hotter. The Boers began to creep gradually nearer. Their front of attack widened and drew around the contours of the hill. Were all the force asleep? On more warning at any rate they should have. Again he darted across the open space with the swish of bullets around him. Again he found the staff. But this time they were annoyed. It is such a bore when young officers are jumpy and alarmist. "It's all right," they said: and so it was within the saucer. The bullets piped overhead as the wind howls outside the well warmed house. But a sudden change impended.

Hamilton rejoined his men just as the Boers attacked at all points. The little picket of Highlanders, utterly unable to withstand the weight of the enemy's advance, ran back to the rim of the saucer intermingled with the Boers, who fired their rifles furiously at them, even putting the muzzles to the men's heads and so destroying them. In Sir William Butler's book, written almost entirely with the view of exonerating Sir George Colley, it is suggested that his advanced picket fell back in a panic. The truth is that they were swept backward by overwhelming force after they had three times reported to the General the development of a heavy attack. Of the seventeen men under Ian Hamilton in this advanced position twelve were shot dead.

The survivors of the picket with the pursuing Boers reached the rum together, and became visible to the main force. Astounded by this apparition, the troops who were lying down in the saucer rose up together, and, some accoutred, some with their coats off, High-landers, sailors, and linesmen, ran forward and fired a ragged volley. A furious musketry fight followed between the Dutch in cover along the rim and the British among the rocks across the centre of the saucer. This was ended by the appearance of other Boers on the high ground at the northern end of the plateau. Without orders or order, exposed to a terrible fire, ignorant of what was required of them, the soldiers wavered. One last chance presented itself. Hamilton rushed up to the General in the impetuosity of youth: "I hope you'll forgive my presumption, sir, but will you let the Gordon Highlanders charge with bayonet?"

"No presumption, young gentleman," replied Colley, with freezing calmness. "We'll let them charge us, and then we'll give them a volley and a charge."

On the word the whole scene broke into splinters. The British troops abandoned their positions and fled from the ground. The Boers, standing up along the rim, shot them down mercilessly — sporting rifles, crack shots, eighty yards' range. Hamilton saw a figure scarcely ten yards away aiming at him, raised his rifle he found himself somehow possessed of to reply. Both fired simultaneously. The British officer went down with his wrist smashed to pieces. He rose again: the rear crest was near. The last of the fugitives were streaming over it. One dash for liberty! The fire was murderous. Before the distance was covered his tunic was cut by one bullet, his knee by another, and finally a splinter of rock striking him behind the head brought him down half stunned to the ground — luckily behind the shelter of a small rock.

The firing stopped. The Boers began to occupy the position. Two discovered the wounded man. The younger, being much excited, would have shot him. The elder restrained him. "Are you officer, you damned Englishman?" said they.

"Yes."

"Give your sword."

Now Hamilton's sword had belonged to his father before him. He replied by offering them money instead.

"Money!" they cried; "give it up at once," and were about to snatch it away when a person in authority — it is said Joubert himself — arrived. "Voorwärts," he said to the burghers, and in spite of their desire to plunder he drove them on. Hamilton thanked him. "This is a bad day for us."

"What can you expect," was the answer characteristic of the Boer — the privileged of God — "from fighting on a Sunday?"

* * *

Then they collected the prisoners and helped Hamilton to walk back to the British position. Colley lay dead on the ground. The Boers would not believe it was the General. "Englishmen are such liars." Hector Macdonald — grim and sad — hero of the Afghan war, now a prisoner in the enemy's hands, watched the proceedings sullenly. The Boers picked out the surrendered prisoners. They looked at Hamilton. He was covered with blood from head to foot. They said: "You will probably die. You may go." So he went; staggered, and crawled back to camp, arrived there delirious the next morning. The wrist joint is composed of eight separate bones. The bullet, breaking through, had disarranged them sadly, had even carried one or two away. If he had consented to amputation he would soon have been convalescent. But a soldier must preserve all he can. What with fever and shock he nearly died. For six months he was an invalid. But the hand was saved, so that now the General can hold an envelope between its paralysed and withered fingers, and sometimes hold a cigarette. For all other purposes it is useless, and when he rides it flaps about helplessly — a glorious deformity.

After some months of doubt as to whether he should leave the army and throw himself entirely into the literary pursuits which had always possessed for him a keen attraction, Hamilton decided to remain a soldier.

He next saw action in the Soudan: he was not intended to make this campaign, for the battalion to which he belonged was serving in India, and there has always been much jealousy between the Indian and the Egyptian British officer. But he happened to be coming home on leave, and when the steamer reached Suez it occurred to him to ask himself why he should not go up the Nile with the columns which were being formed. He got out of the ship accordingly and ran across the sands to the train which was stranding in the station. Had he not caught it he would have returned to the ship. But he was in time. Next day he arrived in Cairo, and while waiting there for his luggage he applied for employment. It was refused, officers were not allowed to volunteer. The Gordon Highlanders, his only hope, had their full complement of officers. They had no vacancy for him. Hamilton did not, however, give up his idea easily. He resolved to travel as far as Wady Halfa and renew his application there. He journeyed south with Colonel Burnaby, and after a week of train and river-boat arrived at the whitewashed mud huts in the midst of a vast circle of sand which marked the base of the British Expeditionary forces, both desert and river columns.

What followed has happened so often that it is well worth the attention of young officers. Be it always remembered that the regulations of the army are formed to make all people quite alike one uniform pattern and on one level of intelligence — not yet the highest. You do not rise by the regulations, but in spite of them. Therefore in all matters of active service the subaltern must never take "No" for an answer. He should get to the front at all costs. For every fifty men who will express a desire to go on service in the mess or the club, and will grumble if they are not selected, there is only about one who really means business and will take the trouble and run the risk of going to the front on the chance. The competition if much less keen when you get there. I know something of this myself, and am convinced of its truth.

The subaltern really stands on velvet in the matter. If he succeeds all is well. If he gets rebuked and ordered down, he must try again. What can the authorities do? They cannot very well shoot him. At the worst they can send him back to his regiment, stop his leave for six months, and some choleric old martinet who was a young man once, though he had half forgotten it, will write in some ponderous book in Pall Mall against the offender's name: "Keen as mustard — takes his own line — to be noted to active service if otherwise qualified."

Of course everyone was delighted to see Hamilton at Wady Halfa. They appointed him to a vacancy which had meanwhile occurred in the Gordon Highlanders, and gave him a company and a boat in the River Column. Through all the hard campaign that followed he served with credit. The fortunes of the troops who worked their way up the Nile have not been so closely studied as those of the columns which plunged into the desert and fought at Abu Klean and Abu Kru. But it was nevertheless one of the most picturesque enterprises of our military history. The broad boats toiling forward against the current of the river, making perhaps three miles a day, obstructed by frequent cataracts and menaced continually by the enemy, the scouts on the banks, the lines of men on the tow ropes, the red sand of the desert, the hot steel sky, and the fierce sunlight slanting in between rocks of the Nile gorge, are materials from which a fascinating sketch might be painted. Hamilton's boat became somehow the head of the rear column. At length there came a day when they were told of expected opposition, dervish encampments, and a certain rocky ridge said to be lined with riflemen. The leading column of boats was hurried forward. By some mischance Hamilton's boat became the lead boat of the leading column. At any rate, his company alone of the Gordon Highlanders fought in the action of Kirbeckan next day. Nothing succeeds like success. Hamilton received the Distinguished Service Order for his services.

After the Nile Expedition of 1885 had reached its sad conclusion, Hamilton returned to India and became an aide-de-camp on the staff of Lord Roberts, who was then commanding the Madras Army. The question of musketry training for infantry was at that time much discussed, and Lord Roberts was determined to do something to improve the shooting of the British army. In his book *Forty-one Years in India* he tells us how he and his staff formed themselves into a team and had many exciting rifle matches with the regiments in the Madras command. In all this, Hamilton's skill with the rifle and the keen interest he had always shown in musketry — his first regimental appointment had been to the Musketry Instructor — stood him in good stead; and when Lord Roberts became Commander-in-Chief in India his aide-de-camp, who had meanwhile served in the Burmah campaign, was made Assistant Adjutant-General for Musketry.

In 1886 he married Jean, daughter of Sir John Muir, Baronet of Deanston, Perthshire. He had now determined to persevere in the military profession, and devoted himself to it with great assiduity. His literary talents were turned to military subjects. He published a book on musketry in the arm entitled *The Fighting of the Future*. It was strong and well written. The introduction of the magazine rifle has modified many of his conclusions, but at the time the book attracted a great deal of attention. He found time, however, to write on other things, and there are still extant from his pen: *A Jaunt in a Junk*, an account of a cruise which he made with his brother down the west coast of Indian; a volume of verses, *The Ballad of Hadji and the Boar*; and one of two other writings. He preserved and extended his acquaintance with literary men, particularly with Andrew Lang, whom he powerfully impressed, and who inscribed a volume of poems to him in the following compulsive lines:

TO COLONEL IAN HAMILTON

To you, who know the face of war,
You, that for England wander far,
You that have seen the Ghazis fly
From English lads not sworn to die,
You that have lain where, deadly chill,
The mist crept o'er the Shameful Hill,
You that have conquered, mile by mile,
The currents of unfriendly Nile,
And cheered the march, and eased the strain
When Politics made valour vain,
Ian, to you, from banks of Ken,
We send out lays of Englishmen!

After doing much useful work in the Musketry Department he became one of the Assistant Quartermaster-Generals in India. From this office he managed to sally forth to the Chitral Expedition, for his services in which on the lines of communication he was made Commander of the Bath. He next became Deputy Quartermaster-General, and it was evident that if he chose to continue to serve in India he would ultimately become the head of the department. In 1897 the Great Frontier War broke out. Hamilton was appointed to command one of the brigades of the Tirah Expeditionary Force. He was at the time on leave in England. He returned at speed, assumed command, and led his brigade through the Kohat Pass in the first movement of the general advance. It looked as if his chance in life had come. He had a magnificent force under him. He enjoyed the confidence of the General-in-chief, Sir William Lockhart, and only a few miles away the enemy awaited the advancing army on the heights of Dargai. The next morning his horse shied suddenly. He was thrown to the ground and broke his leg. They carried the brigadier away in a doolie, his brigade passed to another, and the campaign in Tirah was fought without him.

Ian Hamilton took his bitter disappointment with philosophical composure. "Perhaps," he said to me one day in Calcutta, "I should have lost my reputation had I held my command." But it was easy to see how much he felt the lost opportunity and the enforced inaction. At length his leg mended — after a fashion. He persuaded a medical board to pass him as sound. The campaign continued. There was, however, no vacancy at the front. For several weeks he waited. Presently Sir Bindon Blood — who was preparing for his invasion of Buner, and who knew Hamilton well — applied for him to command his lines of communication. Obstacles were, however, raised by the Indian War Office, and the proposal fell through. At last, in February, when it seemed certain that a spring campaign must be undertaken against the Afridis, Sir William Lockhart decided to replace General Kempster by some other brigadier, and Ian Hamilton was again sent to the front. Afridis gradually paid their toll of rifles, and their jirgahs made submission. The fighting was practically over. Yet in such skirmishing as occurred while Hamilton's brigade was holding the advanced posts in the Bara valley his care and eagerness attracted attention, and, small as was his share of the campaign, Sir William Lockhart gave him an honourable mention in the despatches.

On the restoration of order along the North-West Frontier Hamilton was offered the temporary position of Quartermaster-General in India. Anxious, however, for home employment, and fully alive to the importance of not becoming too closely identified with any particular military set, he declined this important office and proceeded to England on a year's leave. After some delay he was appointed commandant of the School of Musketry at Hythe, and from this post he was twice withdrawn to command brigades at the Manoeuvres. When Sir George White was sent to Natal in September 1899 Hamilton accompanied him as Assistant Adjutant-General. The War Office are therefore entitled to plume themselves upon his successes, for he is one of the few men originally appointed who have increased their reputation.

Ian Hamilton's part in the Boer war is so well known that it will be unnecessary to do more than refer to it here. He displayed a curious facility for handling troops in close contact with the enemy, and practically from the beginning of the fighting he held the command of a brigade. It was Hamilton whose influence went so far to counteract the astounding optimism of the gallant Penn Symons. It was Hamilton who was to have led the bayonet attack by night on the Boer laagers two days before Talana Hill was fought. It was Hamilton to whom French entrusted the entire disposition of the infantry and artillery at Elandslaagte, who arranged the attack, rallied the struggling line, and who led the final charge upon the Boer entrenchment. Again after Lombard's Kop, when the army reeled back in disorder into Ladysmith, it was Hamilton's brigade which, judiciously posted, checked the onset of the victorious enemy. During the defence of Ladysmith Hamilton's section of the defence included Ceasar's Camp and Waggon Hill. He was censured in the Press for not having fortified these positions on their outer crests, and it was said in the army after the 6th of January that this neglect caused unnecessary loss of life. How far this criticism may be just I do not now propose to examine. The arguments against entrenching the outer crest were that heavy works there would draw the enemy's artillery fire, and that the Imperial Light Horse, who were to have defended this section, said they preferred to avail themselves of the natural cover of rocks and stones. The reader would be well advised to defer judgement until some serious and historical work on the campaign in Natal is published. At present all accounts are based on partial and imperfect evidence, nor do I think that the whole true account of a single action has yet been written.

Whatever the rights of this question may be, it is certain that on the 6th January Ian Hamilton, by his personal gallantry and military conduct, restored the situation on Waggon Hill. Indeed, the Homeric contest, when the British General and Commandant Prinsloo of the Free State fired at each other at five yards' range, the fierce and bloody struggle around the embrasure of the naval gun, and the victorious charge of the Devons, may afterwards be found to be the most striking scene in the whole war.

After the relief of Ladysmith, Roberts, who knew where to find the men he wanted, sent for Hamilton, much to the disgust of Sir Redvers Buller, who proposed to keep this good officer for the command of one of his own brigades. On reaching Bloemfontein he was entrusted with the organisation of the mounted infantry division, a post from which he could conveniently be drawn for any service that might be required. Of the rest some account will be found in these letters.

Ian Hamilton is, as the fine portrait by Sargent shows him, a man of rather more than middle height, spare, keen eyed, and of commanding aspect. His highly nervous temperament animating what appears a frail body imparts to all his movements a kind of feverish energy. Two qualities of his mind stand forward prominently from the rest. He is a singularly good and rapid judge of character. He takes a very independent view on all subjects, sometimes with a slight bias towards or affection for their radical and democratic aspects, but never or hardly ever influenced by the set of people with whom he lives. To his strong personal charm as a companion, to his temper never ruffled or vexed either by internal irritation or the stir and contrariness of events, his friends and those who have served under him will bear witness. He has a most happy gift of expression, a fine taste in words, and an acute perception of the curious which he has preserved from his literary days. But it is a whole that we should judge. His mind is built upon a big scale, being broad and strong, capable of thinking in army corps and if necessary in continents, and working always with serene smoothness undisturbed alike by responsibility or danger. Add to all this a long experience in war, high military renown both for courage and conduct, the entire confidence and affection of the future Commander-in-Chief, the luck that has carried him through so many dangers, and the crowning advantage of being comparatively young, and it is evident that here is a man who in the years that are to come will have much to do with the administration of the British Army in times of peace and its direction in the field.

CHAPTER NINE

THE ACTION OF HOUTNEK

Winburg: May 8

Ian Hamilton's orders were to march north from Thabanchu on Winburg by the Jacobsrust road, and he was expected, if not opposition was encountered, to reach his destination by the 7th of May. The column with which he started from Thabanchu was composed of Smith-Dorrien's 19th Infantry Brigade, Ridley's Mounted Infantry Brigade, and two batteries of artillery; but at Jacobsrust he would receive a strong reinforcement, consisting of Bruce-Hamilton's 21st Brigade of Infantry, Broadwood's Cavalry Brigade, two batteries of field and one of horse artillery, and two 5-in. guns. The accession would raise his force to a total of 7,500 infantry, 4,000 mounted men, and thirty-two guns — an imposing command for an officer who had not yet had time to take the badges of a colonel off his shoulders. The first thing, however, was to reach Jacobsrust, and effect the junction with Bruce-Hamilton's force.

The Thabanchu column started at daybreak on the 30th of April, and when it was within three or four miles of Houtnek Poort the enemy suddenly unmasked field guns and "pom-poms", and opened a long-range fire with them from the east on the right flank of the marching troops. Colonel Bainbridge, with the 7th Corps of mounted infantry, wheeled up to contain this force of the enemy, and at the same time De Lisle — of polo fame — pushed forward boldly at a gallop with the 6th Corps and the New Zealanders, and seized a commanding position about 2,000 yards south of the actual nek. Colonel Legge, meanwhile advancing on the left front, noticed that Thoba Mountain was weakly held by the enemy, and thereupon ordered Kitchener's Horse to attack it, thus anticipating the order which the General was himself about to send. These dispositions, which were made on their own initiative by the various mounted infantry officers, enabled a deliberate view of the situation to be taken.

The pass of Houtnek consists of two parallel grassy ridges separated by a smooth shallow valley a little more than a mile across, and devoid of cover. On the east the pass runs up into sharp rocky kopjes, strengthened by successive lines of stone walls trailing away towards the main laagers of the enemy. Both the centre and the left flank of the Boer position refused all opportunity to attack. The

Dutch right was scarcely more encouraging. On the west of the pass rose the great mountain of Thoba, an uneven battlefield, better suited to Boers than to British troops. Yet as it was on Hamilton's safer flank, dominated the rest of the enemy's position, could be turned by mounted troops making a very wide detour, and being, moreover, the only way, the General resolved to attack it.

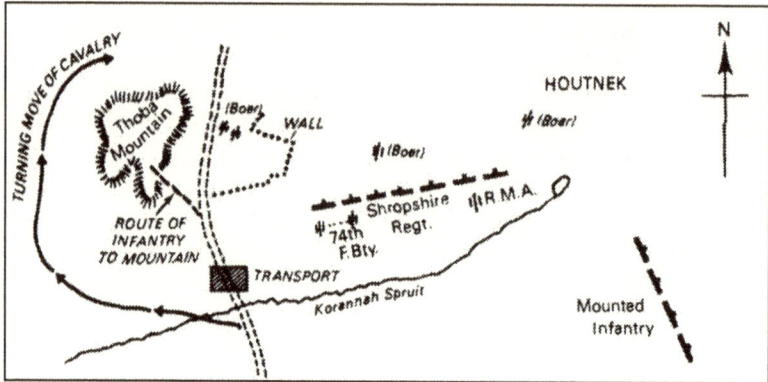

At 9:30 the infantry began to come up, and at ten o'clock the approaches to the Boer position were strongly occupied. As soon as Kitchener's Horse were seen to have made good their footing on Thoba Mountain, Hamilton ordered General Smith-Dorrien to support them with part of their brigade, which was accordingly done, two companies of the Shropshires, the Gordon Highlanders, and four companies of the Canadians being successively worked up on to the hill under a heavy shell fire from the enemy. This practically disposed of the whole force, which was soon engaged all along the line, the mounted infantry holding the enemy off the right and right rear, the Cornwalls guarding the baggage, one-half Smith-Dorrien's Brigade containing the front, and the other half with Kitchener's Horse pushing the flank attack on Thoba Mountain.

As soon as the Boers understood the designs of the British on Thoba they made a strong effort to regain and hold that important feature. At first the troops made good progress; but as the enemy received continual reinforcements the resistance became more severe, until, presently, far from gaining ground, they began to lose it. At last, about two o'clock, some one hundred and fifty of the German corps of the Boer force advanced from the northern point of Thoba in four lines across the table top to drive the British off the hill. So regular was their order that it was not until their levelled rifles were seen pointing south that they were recognised as foes, and artillery opened on them. In spite of an accurate shell fire they continued to advance boldly against the highest part of the hill, and, meanwhile, cloaked by a swell of the ground, Captain Towse, of the Gordon Highlanders, with twelve men of his own regiment and ten of Kitchener's Horse, was steadily moving towards them. The scene on the broad stage of the Thoba plateau was intensely dramatic. The whole army were the witness.

The two forces, strangely disproportioned, drew near to each other. Neither was visible to the other. The unexpected collision impended. From every point field glasses were turned on the spectacle, and even hardened soldiers held their breath. At last, with suddenness, both parties came face to face at fifty yards' distance. The Germans, who had already made six prisoners, called loudly on Captain Towse and his little band to surrender. What verbal answer was returned is not recorded; but a furious splutter of musketry broke out at once, and in less than a minute the long lines of the enemy recoiled in confusion, and the top of the hill was secured to the British. Among the foreigners wounded in this encounter was Colonel Maximoff.

Captain Towse, for his conspicuous gallantry, and for the extraordinary results which attended it, has been rewarded the Victoria Cross; but, in gaining what is above all things precious to a soldier, he lost what is necessary to a happy life, for in the moment when his military career was assured by a brilliant feat of arms, it was terminated by a bullet which, striking him sideways, blinded him in both eyes. Thus do Misery and Joy walk hand in hand on the field of war.

All this time the rifle and gun fire along the whole front had been continuous, and as the day wore on without the British making good their hold on Thoba Mountain the enemy gathered in a more and more threatening attitude on the right of the column, and by four o'clock at least 1,500 men were collected, with guns and "pom-poms", which threw shell into the rearguard and transport. Hamilton, however, was determined to fight the matter out. He therefore directed that all troops should post guards on their front, lie down wherever darkness found them, and prepare to renew the action by daybreak. He then telegraphed to General French for some assistance, the need of more mounted troops being painfully felt.

At dawn on May-day fighting recommenced, and soon after six o'clock parties of the Gordons and Canadians succeeded in gaining possession of the two peaks of Thoba Mountain. Besides this, half a company of the Shropshires, under Colour-Sergeant Sconse, managed to seize the nek between them, and though subjected to a severe cross-fire, which caused in this small party ten casualties out of forty, maintained themselves stubbornly for four hours. The points which dominated the flat top of the mountain were thus gained.

Meanwhile reinforcements, consisting of the 8th Hussars, a composite Lancer regiment, the East Yorkshires, and a field battery, had arrived from Thabanchu, and the approach of Bruce-Hamilton's force from the direction of Kranz Kraal was also felt. General Ian Hamilton now ordered Colonel Clowes, commanding the Cavalry, to move right round Thoba Mountain and threaten the Boer line of retreat as a preliminary and accompaniment of the main Infantry assault, which had now become inevitable. Clowes's force was strengthened by the addition of a horse battery. The newly-arrived Infantry and the field battery had to be diverted to support the right and right rear, where the pressure was now very strong.

At about 8 a.m. General Smith-Dorrien had himself gone up to the top of Thoba Mountain to direct personally the decisive movement when the time should come. A little before one o'clock, the progress of the Cavalry being satisfactory, he determined to settle the matter, so that if necessary the force might get its baggage over the pass before dark. He therefore formed a line of infantry right across the plateau, two companies of the Shropshires in the centre, and one and a half companies of the Gordons on either flank. The advance was sounded.

The troops moved forward with alacrity. For a few moments the fire was heavy, but the Boers knew themselves bested, and on the soldiers raising the cheer that precedes the actual assault they rushed to their horses, and the whole of Thoba Mountain was won. The rest of the position now became untenable, and the enemy, to the number of 4,000, promptly evacuated it, galloping swiftly back in the direction of Jacobsrust.

A few troops of the 8th Hussars alone got near enough to charge; half-a-dozen Dutchmen were sabred, and one was shot dead by an officer, Lieutenant Wylam. The Boers who were making the attack on the right retreated at the same time as their comrades, and the transport, no longer molested, passed safely over the pass and parked for the night on the northern side. No trustworthy estimate can be formed of the enemy's loss; but a score of prisoners were taken, and an equal number of bodies were found on the position.

The British casualties were fortunately slight considering the fire and its duration, and did not exceed a hundred officers and men.

The next day the junction between the columns was effected

and Ian Hamilton's force formed, with reference to the main advance, the Army of the Right Flank, and was composed as follows (for full composition, see Appendix):

Infantry	19th Brigade	Smith-Dorrien
	21st Brigade	Bruce-Hamilton
Mounted Infantry	1st M.I. Brigade	Ridley
Cavalry	2nd Cavalry Brigade	Broadwood
Artillery	3 Batteries F.A. \	
	2 Batteries H.A. —	Waldron
	2 five-in. Guns /	

The force was supported by the Highland Brigade and two 4.7 naval guns, under General Colvile, who was directed to follow the leading column at a distance of ten miles. Hamilton proposed to march forward on the 2nd of May, but an order from headquarters enjoined a halt; nor was it until the afternoon of the 3rd that the force reached Jacobsrust, as it is called by the inhabitants, Isabellasfontein, as the maps record. A little cavalry skirmishing in the neighborhood of the camp resulted in the death of one Lancer.

On the 4th of May the whole army moved forward again, Lord Roberts passing through Brandfort towards Smaldeel, Hamilton continuing his march on Winburg. This day did not pass without fighting, for scarcely had the troops left camp when a patter of musketry warned the General that his cavalry had become engaged. Riding forward, he was the witness of a very dashing cavalry exploit. Across the line of advance was drawn up a strong force of the enemy, estimated at 4,000 men and thirteen guns. These, in a good position along a range of wooded bluffs, promised a sufficient task for the troops during the day. But now, suddenly, from the direction of Brandfort, a new army of Boers began to appear, riding swiftly down to join hands with their comrades athwart the road, and fall on the left flank of the column.

The thing was urgent, and perhaps vital. But between the fast converging Boer forces, at the angle where they would meet, ran a long ridge of indefinite extent. General Broadwood at once, without a moment's delay, galloped forward, and with two squadrons of the Guard's Cavalry and two of the 10th Hussars seized it. The Boers were already scrambling up its lower slopes. A sharp fight immediately opened. Kitchener's Horse, hurrying up in support, occupied a further point of the ridge, and the Dutch, after a determined but futile attempt to clear the hill, fell back. The junction of the two

Boer columns was prevented. It seems that the whole of their plan for the day was based on this first condition, and in an army where every individual soldier must have the details of any plan explained to him it is not easy to make fresh dispositions in the field.

Indeed, a sort of panic seems to have taken hold of the enemy, for without waiting for the infantry attack to develop they fled forthwith at great speed, galloping madly across the drift — as the British proprietor of Welcome Farm told me — horsemen and guns, pell-mell, in downright rout, pursued, so swift was their departure, only by the shells of the horse artillery.

Those losses in this brief affair were not large, and almost entirely among the cavalry. In those few minutes of firing on the ridge about a dozen troopers had been hit. Lord Airlie was slightly wounded in the arm, and Lieutenant Rose, Royal Horse Guards, was killed. He had been sent forward to see what lay beyond the further crest of the hill, and found that deadly riflemen lay there waiting for a certain victim. He fell pierced by several bullets, and lived only half an hour.

This officer was a most zealous solider. Though possessed of private means which would have enabled him to lead a life of ease and pleasure, he had for several years devoted himself assiduously to the military profession. He went to India as a volunteer during the Tirah Campaign, and served with distinction on Sir Penn Symon's staff — general and aide-de-camp both vanished now, as the foam fades in the wake of a fast ship! From India he hastened to West Africa, and in that vile and pestilential region won a considerable reputation; indeed, he was to have received the Distinguished Service Order for his part in recent operations there had not another war intervened. He arrived at the Cape scarcely a month ago, full of hope and energy. This is the end; and while it is one which a soldier must be ready to meet, deep sympathy will be felt for the father, from whom the public necessities have now required two gallant sons.

Though the disorderly and demoralised nature of the Boer flight through Welcome Farm was known throughout the British Army, it was not expected that so strong a position as the bluffs behind the Vet River would be yielded without a shot fired. This, nevertheless, proved to be the case, for when, on the morning of the 6th, Hamilton resumed his advance, he found that no force of the enemy stood before him and Winburg.

He therefore sent, shortly after noon, a staff officer, Captain Balfour to wit, under flag of truce, with a letter to the mayor of the town summoning him forthwith to surrender the town and all stores therein, and promising that if this were done he would use every effort to protect property, and that whatever food-stuffs were required by the troops should be paid for. This message, which was duly heralded by the sound of a trumpet, concluded by saying that unless an acceptance was received within two hours the General would understand that this offer had been declined.

Thus accredited, Captain Balfour made his way into the town and was soon the centre of an anxious and excited crowd of burghers and others who filled the market square. The mayor, the landdrost, and other prominent persons — indeed, all the inhabitants — were eager to avail themselves of the good terms, and a satisfactory settlement was almost arranged when, arriving swiftly from the north-east, Philip Botha and a commando of 500 men, mostly Germans and Hollanders, all very truculent since they were as yet unbeaten, entered the town.

A violent and passionate scene ensued. Botha declared he would never surrender Winburg without a fight. Dissatisfied with the attentions paid him by Captain Balfour, he turned furiously on him and rated him soundly. Several of the Free Staters had asked what would be done to them if they laid down their arms. Balfour had replied that they would be permitted to return to their farms, unless actually captured on the field. This Botha held to be a breach of the laws of war, and he thereupon charged the officer with attempting to suborn his burghers. What had he to say that he should not be made a prisoner? "I ask no favours of no Dutchman," replied Balfour, sternly.

"Arrest that man!" shouted Botha, in a fury; "I shall begin shooting soon." At these shameful words a great commotion arose. The women screamed, the mayor and landdrost rushed forward in the hopes of averting bloodshed. The Boers raised their rifles in menace, and the unarmed British envoy flourished his white flag indignantly.

For several minutes it seemed that an actual scuffle, possible a tragedy, would occur. But the influence of the townsfolk, who knew that their liberty and property lay in the hands of the Imperial General, and that the great siege guns were even then being dragged into effective range, prevailed, and Philip Botha, followed by his men, galloped furiously from the square towards the north.

That afternoon General Ian Hamilton entered Winburg at the head of his troops. Under a shady tree outside the town the mayor and landdrost tendered their submission and two large silver keys. The Union Jack was hoisted in the market-place amid the cheers of the British section of the inhabitants, and, as each battalion marching through the streets saw the famous emblem of pride and power, bright in the rays of the setting sun, these feeble or interested plaudits were drowned in the loud acclamations of the victorious invaders.

Hamilton was expected to arrive on the 7th, if no opposition was encountered. He had fought nearly every day, and reached the town of the evening of the 5th.

CHAPTER TEN

THE ARMY OF THE RIGHT FLANK

Kroonstadt: May 16, 1900

On the same day that Ian Hamilton's force won their fight at Houtnek, to wit, the 1st of May, the advance of the main army towards Pretoria, long expected, long prepared, long delayed, began, and the Eleventh Division marched north from Bloemfontein to join the Seventh, which was entrenched at Karree Siding. On the 3rd both infantry divisions moved forward along the railway, their left protected by Gordon's Cavalry Brigade and Hutton's Mounted Infantry, and after a sharp cannonade drove the Boers from their positions covering Brandfort and entered the town. The advance was resumed on the 5th, and the enemy were again met with, this time holding the line of the Vet River. Another artillery action ensued, in which the British 5-inch and naval 4.7 guns were very effective, and at the end of which the West Australians and other parts of Hutton's Mounted Infantry force, pushed across the river in gallant style and captured an important kopje. The Dutchmen then retreated, and the Field-Marshal's headquarters on the 6th were fixed in Smaldeel. His losses since leaving Bloemfontein had not amounted to twenty-five men.

Ian Hamilton, in spite of the long marches his troops had made, was impatient to push on from Winburg without delay, and, following the track to Ventersburg, to seize the drifts across the Sand River, twenty miles to the north. The great speed of his last movement had outpaced the Boers, and their convoys were struggling along abreast of, and even behind, the British column, trying vainly to slip across our front, and join the burgher forces accumulating for the defence of Kroonstadt. By marching forthwith — great though the strain might be — the General hoped to secure the bloodless passage of the river, and perhaps cut up some of these same toiling convoys. Accordingly, having collected from the town about three days' stores — Sir Henry Colvile helping him unselfishly with mule waggons — he set his brigades in motion on the afternoon of the 6th, and marched nine miles towards the Sand.

But Lord Roberts had decided to remain at Smaldeel until his temporary bridge over the Vet River was made and the trains running, and he did not choose to run the risk of the Boers concentrating all their forces upon any single division of his army, such as would be incurred if Hamilton pushed forward alone. The principle was indisputable; but, of course, in practice it resolved itself into another instance of balancing drawbacks, for delay gave the enemy time to get his breath, and meant that the Sand River passage would be opposed. Besides, if the Boers had flung all their strength upon Hamilton, we were 7,000 bayonets; 3,000 horse; and nearly forty guns, and would have beat them off with a shocking slaughter. To us it seemed a great pity to wait; but to the Chief, in whose eyes the Army of the Right Flank was but one column of that far-flung line which stretched from Rundle near Senekal, along the front of the main army to Methuen near Boshof, Hunter at Warrenton, and Mahon far away on the fringe of the Kalahari desert, it must have been a very small matter, and certainly not one justifying any loss of cohesion in the general scheme. So I have no doubt that it was right to make us halt on the 7th and 8th.

On the former of these two days of rest Lord Roberts sent for General Hamilton to meet him at a point on the branch railway line midway between Winburg and Smaldeel, and they had a long private conference together. On the 9th, the whole army marched forward again toward the Sand River. I rode with the General, who managed somehow to find himself among the cavalry patrols of the right flank guard; and we watched with telescopes three long lines of dust in the eastward, which, under examination, developed into horsemen and waggons marching swiftly north and turning more and more across our front. It was clear that if we had pushed on without halting, all these commandos would have been prevented from reaching Kroonstadt. The General contemplated them hungrily for some time, but they were too far off to attack, bearing in mind the great combination of which we were a part. The flanking patrols, however, exchanged a few shots.

The march was not a long one, and by mid-day we reached the halting-place, a mile south of the river. The headquarters were fixed in a large farm which stood close to the waggon track we followed.

This farmhouse was certainly the best purely Dutch homestead I have ever seen in the 500 miles I have ridden about the Free State. It was a large square building, with a deep verandah, and a pretty flower-garden in front, and half a dozen barns and stables around it. The construction of a dam across the neighbouring spruit had formed a wide and pleasant pool, in which many good fat ducks and geese were taking refuge from the wandering soldier. At the back, indeed, on all sides but the front of the farm, rose a thick belt of fir-trees. Within the house the ground-floor was divided into three excellent bedrooms, with old-fashioned feather-beds and quaint wooden bedsteads, a prim but spacious parlour, a kitchen, pantry, and store-room. The parlour deserved the greatest attention. The furniture was dark and massive. The boards of the floor were deeply stained. In the middle was a good carpet upon which an ample oval table stood. The walls were hung with curious prints of coloured plates, and several texts in Dutch. One pair of plates I remembered represented the ten stages of man's life and woman's life, and showed both in every period from the cradle to the grace, which latter was not reached until the comfortable age of one hundred. The woman's fortunes were especially prosperous. At birth she sprawled contentedly in a cradle, whilst loving parents bent over her in rapture, and dutiful angles hung attendant in the sky. At ten she scampered after a hoop. At twenty she reclined on the stalwart shoulder of an exemplary lover. At thirty she was engaged in teaching *seven* children their letters. At forty, she celebrated a silver wedding. At fifty, still young and blooming, she attended the christening of a grandchild. At sixty, it was a great-grandchild. At seventy she enjoyed a golden wedding. At eighty she was smilingly engaged in knitting. Even at ninety she was well preserved, nor could she with reason complain of her lot in life when, at a hundred, the inevitable hour arrived. "Be fruitful and multiply", was the meaning of a Dutch text on the opposite wall, and a dozen children black and white (little Kaffirs, the offspring of the servants, playing with the sons and daughters of the house) showed that the spirit of the injunction was observed; and these are things with which the statesman will have to reckon.

The inmates of the farm consisted of the old man, a venerable gentleman of about sixty years, his dame, a few years younger, three grown-up daughters, a rather ill-favoured spinster sister, and seven or eight children or grandchildren of varying ages. There were in all seven sons or grandsons — two were married and had farms of their own; but all, including even one of fourteen, were "on commando" at the wars, some, perhaps, looking at us and their home from the heights across the river.

The General politely requested shelter for the night, and a bedroom and the parlour were placed at his disposal; not very enthusiastically, indeed, but that was only natural. The staff settled down in the verandah so as not to disturb the family. Ian Hamilton, keenly interested in everything, began at once to ask the old lady questions through an interpreter. She gave him answers with no good grace, and when the General inquired about her youngest fighting son — he of fourteen — her sour face showed signs of emotion, and the conversation ended for the day. On the morrow, however, just before he crossed the river, he had to come back to the telegraph-tent pitched near the farm, and found time to see her again.

"Tell her," he said to the interpreter, "that we have won the battle to-day."

They told her, and she bowed her head with some dignity.

"Tell her that the Dutch will now certainly be beaten in the war."

No response.

"Perhaps her sons will be taken prisoners."

No answer.

"Now tell her to write down on a piece of paper the names of the youngest, and give it to my aide-de-camp; and then when he is captured she must write to me or to the Hoofd-General, and we will send him back to her, and not keep him a prisoner."

She thawed a little at this, and expressed a hope that he had been comfortable while beneath her roof, and then — for the guns were still firing — he had to hurry away. But the aide-de-camp remained behind for the paper.

During the time we spent in this homely place I made a thorough inspection of the farm, especially the parlour, where I found one very curious book. It was a collection of national songs and ballads, compiled, and in part written, by Mr. Reitz. I afterwards succeeded in buying another copy in Ventersburg; indeed, it has been widely disseminated. The first part consists of patriotic Boer poems — the Volkslied, the Battle of Majuba, the Battle of Laing's Nek, and other similar themes. The second half of the book is filled with Reitz's translations of English songs and well-known ditties into the *taal*. John Gilpin, besides being a burgher of credit and renown, was eke a Field-Cornet of famous Bloemfontein. Young Lochinvar had come from out of the Boshof district. The Laanndrost's daughter of Winburg found a lover no less faithful than a famous swain of Islington. The pictures were mightily diverting. The old Field Cornet Gilpin   "Jan Jurgens", as he called himself now — was shown galloping wildly along, on a pulling Basuto pony, through the straggling streets of, let us say, Ventersburg, his slough hat crammed over his eyes, his white beard flapping in the wind, while a stately *vrouw*, four children, and a Kaffir, flung up their hands in mingled wonder and derision.

One piece began:

> Engels! Engels! alles Engels! Engels wat jij siet en hoor.
> Ins ons skole, in ons kerke, word ons modertaal vermoor.

I cannot read Dutch, but the meaning and object of the book were sufficiently clear without that knowledge.

F. W. Reitz, sometimes President of the Free State, now State Secretary of the Transvaal, looked far ahead, and worked hard. This, the foundation-stone of the vernacular literature, was but one act in the long scheme of policy, pursued, year in year out, with tireless energy, and indomitable perseverance, to manufacture a new Dutch nation in South Africa — the policy which, in the end, had brought a conquering army to this quiet farm, and scattered the schemers far and wide. But what a game it must have been to play! Only a little more patience, a little less pride and over-confidence, concessions here, concessions there, anything to gain time, and then, some day — a mighty Dutch Republic, "the exchange of a wealthier Amsterdam, the schools of a more learned Leyden", and, above all — no cursed Engels.

I was considering these matters, only suggested here, when messengers and the sound of firing came in from the eastward. The news that small parties of Boers were engaging our right flank guard did not prevent Hamilton riding over to meet the Chief, nor tempt us to quit the cool verandah of the farm; but when, suddenly, at about three o'clock, fifty shots rang out in quick succession, scarcely 500 yards away, every one got up in a hurry, and snatching pistols and belts, ran out to see what mischance had occurred. The scene that met out eyes was unusual. Down the side of the hill there poured a regular cascade of antelope — certainly not less that 700 or 800 in number — maddened with fear at finding themselves in the midst of the camp, and seeking frantically for a refuge. This spectacle, combined with the hope of venison, was too much for the soldiers, and forthwith a wild and very dangerous fire broke out, which was not stopped until fifteen or twenty antelopes were killed, and one Australian mounted infantryman wounded in the stomach, The injury of the latter was at first thought to be serious, and the rumour ran that he was dead; but, luckily, the bullet only cut the skin.

Thus disturbed, I thought it might be worth while to walk up to the outpost line and see what was passing there. When I reached the two guns which were posted on the near ridge, the officers were in consultation. Away across the Sand River, near two little kopjes, was a goodly Boer commando. They had just arrived from the east of our line of march, and having skirted round our pickets had set themselves down to rest and refresh. Spread as they were on the smooth grass, the telescope showed every detail. There were about 150 horsemen, with five ox-waggons and two guns. The horses were grazing, but not off-saddled. The men were lying or sitting on the ground. Evidently they thought themselves out of range. The subaltern commanding the guns was not quite sure that he agreed with them. Some Colonial mounted infantry officers standing near were almost indignant that the guns should let such a chance slip. The subaltern was very anxious to fire — "really think I could reach the brutes"; but he was afraid he would get into trouble if he fired his guns at any range greater than artillery custom approves. His range finders said "6,000". Making allowances for the clear atmosphere, I should have thought it was more. At last he decided to have a shot. "Sight in for 5,600, and let's see how much we fall short." The gun cocked its nose high in the air and flung its shell accordingly. To our astonishment the projectile passed far over the Boer commando, and burst nearly 500 yards beyond them: to our astonishment and to theirs. The burghers lost no time in changing their position. The men ran to their horses, and, mounting, galloped away in a dispersing cloud. Their guns whipped up and made for the further hills. The ox-waggons sought the shelter of a neighbouring donga. Meanwhile, the artillery subaltern, delighted at the success of his venture, pursued all these objects with his fire, and using both his guns threw at least a dozen shells among them. Material result: one horse killed. This sort of artillery fire is what we call waste of ammunition when we do it to others, and a confounded nuisance when they do it to us. After all, who is there who enjoys being disturbed by shells just as he is settling himself comfortably to rest, after a long march? And who fights the better next day for having to scurry a mile and a half to cover with iron pursuers at their heels? Even as it was an opportunity was lost. We ought to have sneaked up six guns, a dozen if there were a dozen handy, all along the ridge, and let fly with the whole lot, at ranges varying from 5,000 to 6,000 yards with time shrapnel. Then there would have been a material as well as a moral effect. "Pooh," says the scientific artillerist, "you would have used fifty shells, tired your men, and disturbed your horses, to hit a dozen scallawags and stampede 150. That is not the function of artillery." Nevertheless function or no function, it is war, and the way to win war. Harass, bait, and worry your enemy until you establish a funk. Once he is more frightened of you than you are of him, all your enterprises will prosper; and if fifty shells can in any way accelerate that happy condition, be sure they are not wasted.

The afternoon passed uneventfully away, though the outposts were gradually drawn into a rifle duel with the Dutch sharpshooters in the scrub across the river. In the evening the General returned from his conference with Lord Roberts, and told us the passage was to be forced on the morrow all along the line. The Army of the Right Flank would cross by the nearest drift in our present front. The Seventh Division inclining to its right would come into line on our left. The Field-Marshal, with the Guards and the rest of Pole-Carew's Division, would strike north along the line of the railway. French, with two cavalry brigades and Hutton's Mounted Infantry Brigade, was to swing around the enemy's right and push hard for Ventersburg siding. Broadwood from our flank, with the Second Cavalry Bridage, and such of the Second Mounted Infantry Brigade as could be spared, was to be thrust through as soon as the Boer front was broken, and try to join hands with French, thus, perhaps, cutting off and encircling the Boer right. The diagram — it is not a map — below will help to explain the scheme.

The operation of the next day was one of the largest and most extended movements of the war, although, probably from this cause, it was attended by very little loss of life. Upon the British side

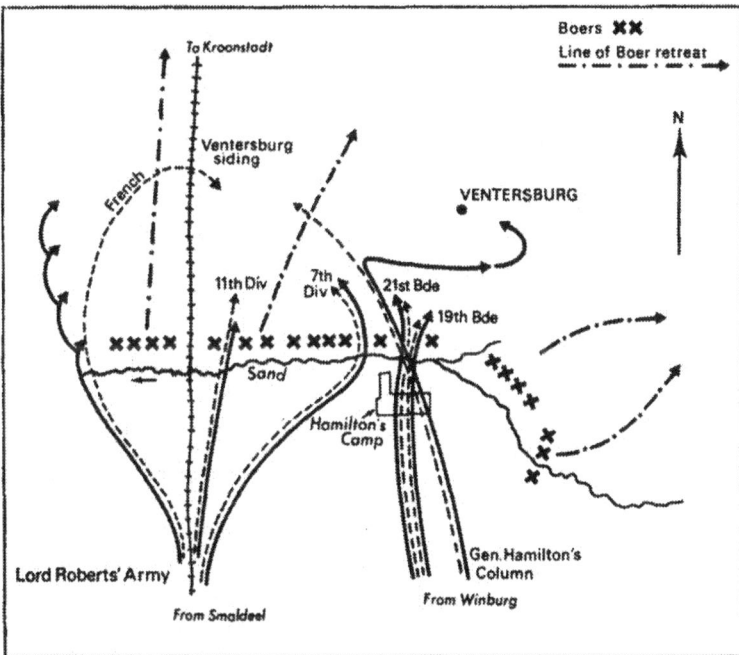

DIAGRAM TO EXPLAIN THE PASSAGE OF THE
SAND RIVER, 10TH OF MAY, 1900
The dotted lines show what was proposed; the
continuous lines show what was done
The crosses indicate the Boers

six infantry and six mounted brigades, with rather more than 100 guns, were brought into action along a front of over twenty-five miles. The Boers, however, still preserved their flanks. Upon the west they succeeded in holding up French, and on the east they curled round Hamilton's right and rear so that his action here, which in its early stages resembled that afterwards fought at Diamond Hill, was of a piercing rather than a turning nature. But in thus amazingly extending their scanty forces, which, altogether, did not number more than 9,000 men, with twenty-five guns, the enemy became so weak all along their front that the attacking divisions broke through everywhere, as an iron bar might smash thin ice, with scarcely any shock.

On the evening of the 10th, the British forces, in their extended line, lay spread along the south bank of the river, just out of cannon-shot of the Boer positions on the further side. French, indeed, did not rest content with securing his ford twelve miles to the west of the railway, but pushed his two brigades across before dark. The wisdom of this movement is disputed. On the one hand, it is contended that by crossing he revealed the intention of the Commander-in-Chief, and drew more opposition against himself the next day. On the other, it is urged that he was right to get across unopposed while he could, and that his purpose was equally revealed, no matter which side of the river he stayed. During the night Ian Hamilton, at the other end of the line, seized the drift in his front with a battalion, which promptly entrenched itself. Tucker, who proposed to cross near the same point, despatched the Cheshire Regiment for a similar purpose. The single battalion was sufficient; but the importance and wisdom of the movement was proved by the fact that the enemy during the night sent 400 men to occupy the river bank and hold the passage, and found themselves forestalled.

At daybreak the engagement was begun along the whole front. I am only concerned with Ian Hamilton's operations, but, in order that these may be understood, some mention must be made of the other forces. French advanced as soon as it was light, and almost immediately became engaged with a strong force of Boers, who barred his path, and prevented his closing on the railway as intended. A sharp cavalry action followed, in which the Boers fought with much stubbornness; and the Afrikander Horse, a corps of formidable mercenaries, even came to close quarters with Dickson's brigade, and were charged. French persevered through the day, making very little progress towards the railway, but gaining ground gradually to the north. Although his casualties numbered more than a hundred, he was still some distance from Ventersburg sliding at nightfall. The centre attack properly awaited the progress of the flanking movements, and was, during the early part of the day, contented with an artillery bombardment, chiefly conducted by its heavy guns. Tucker and Hamilton, however, fell on with much determination, and were soon briskly engaged.

Ian Hamilton began his action at half-past five, with his heavy guns, which shelled the opposite heights leisurely, while the infantry and cavalry were moving off. The Boer position before us ran along a line of grassy ridges, with occasional kopjes, which sloped up gradually and reached their summits about a mile from the river. But besides this position, which was the objective of the force, the Boers, who held all the country to the east, began a disquieting

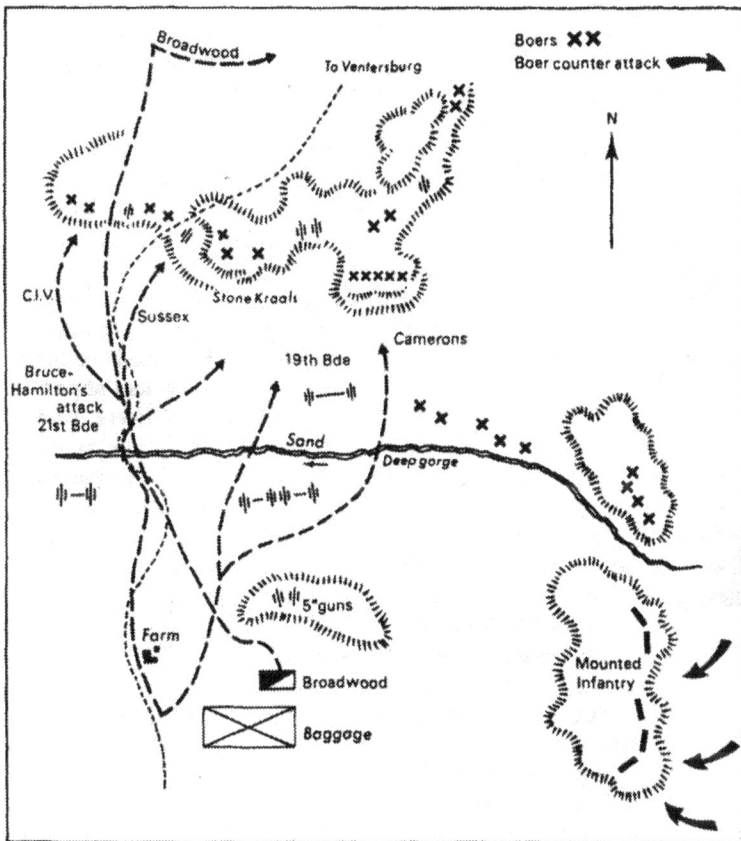

IAN HAMILTON'S ACTION AT THE SAND RIVER,
10TH OF MAY, 1900
The crosses indicate the Boers

attack along our right and right rear, and although the mounted infantry, and principally Kitchener's Horse, under Major Fowle, held them at arm's length throughout the day, the firing in this quarter caused the General some concern, and occupied the greater part of his attention.

At six o'clock the Twenty-first Brigade began to cross the river, and Bruce-Hamilton, stretching out to his left, soon developed a wide front. The Boers now opened fire with two or three field-guns and a "pom-pom", which latter was quickly silenced by our heavy pieces. At the same time, the Nineteenth Brigade, who were containing the enemy's left, became engaged with their skirmishers in the scrub by the river. The four batteries of field artillery also came into action, and were pushed forward across the drift as soon as sufficient space was gained by the Infantry. At a little after seven the head of General Tucker's Division appeared on the plain to our left, and that determined officer trust his men over the river in most vigorous style. Moreover, seeing Bruce-Hamilton committed to an assault, he swung two of his own batteries round to the eastward, and so rendered us material assistance.

Both Smith-Dorrien, who directed the two infantry brigades, and Ian Hamilton were fully alive to the grave dangers of crowding too many troops on to a narrow front, and the infantry attack was very sparingly fed with supports, until it became completely extended. This condition was attained about eleven o'clock, when the Camerons were sent across the river to clear the scrub and prolong the line to the right. Bruce-Hamilton now had his deployment completed, and with an admirable simultaneity the whole of the assaulting Infantry rose up and advanced together upon the enemy's position, covered by the heavy fire of twenty-six guns. The panorama was now very extensive. Far away to the left the smoke of lyddite shells, and the curious speck of the war-balloon high in the clear air, showed that the centre was engaged. The whole of the Seventh Division had crossed the Sand, and were now curving to the north-west amid a crackle of fire. Before us the slopes were sprinkled with brown dots moving swiftly upwards. The crest of the ridge was fringed with exploding shells. For a few minutes the Boers fired steadily, and the dust jumped amid the Sussex Regiment and the City Imperial Volunteers. But both infantry and artillery attacks were far beyond the capacity of the defence to resist, and by noon the whole of the heights beyond the Sand were in British possession.

Ian Hamilton had meanwhile ordered baggage and cavalry to cross. Broadwood was over the enemy's position almost as soon as the infantry. He proceeded to move in the direction of Ventersburg siding. The enemy, however, had covered themselves with a strong rearguard, and the cavalry were soon opposed by three guns and a force of riflemen of considerable numbers. Whether Broadwood would have thought it worth while to make here the effort which he afterwards made in the action of Diamond Hill, and order a charge, is uncertain; for at this moment a misunderstanding arose which induced him to change his plans altogether.

The Boer pressure on our right rear had been growing stronger and stronger all the morning, and at length Hamilton, wishing to check the enemy sharply, so as to draw his rearguard over the river after his baggage, told his chief of artillery to find him a battery. Now it happened that only one of the two horse batteries, P, had been able to go with the Cavalry, the other, Q, being too tried to keep up. The chief of artillery therefore proposed to send for the tired battery. Unfortunately, by some mistake, either in giving or taking the order, the orderly was sent for P instead of Q. The man, a sergeant-major, galloped across the river, and, understanding that the matter was urgent, hurried after Broadwood, overtook him, who knew that Hamilton would never deprive him of his guns except for some very urgent reason, sent them at once, abandoned his movement to the north-west, which indeed was now impracticable without artillery, and concluding that the rearguard was seriously involved, turned sharply to the east to assist them. Explanations arrived too late to make it worth while to revert to the original plan, and, perhaps, seeing that French was unable to make Ventersburg siding, it was just as well that Broadwood did not try alone.

Broadwood's latest movement, or the action of the artillery, or the knowledge that the British had successfully forced the passage of the river at all points, induced the Boers who were assailing the rearguard to desist, and the musketry in that quarter gradually died away. Meanwhile, by the exertions of Lieutenant-Colonel Maxse, the baggage had mostly been dragged across the river, and Ian Hamilton made haste to overtake his victorious Infantry, who had already disappeared into the valley beyond the enemy's position. By the time that we reached the top of the high ground, Bruce-Hamilton's leading battalions were vanishing in a high cloud of dust to the eastward. The City Imperial Volunteers, who had lost a few men in the attack, were resting on the hill after their advance, and eating their biscuits. Several dead Boers had been found lying among the rocks, and a burial party was at work digging a grave for these and for four of our own men who had fallen close by. There were also a few prisoners — Transvaalers for the mot part — who had surrendered when the troops fixed bayonets. Four miles away to the north-east the trees and houses of Ventersburg rose from a grassy hollow.

The General decided to bivouac in the valley beyond the enemy's position, and to set his pickets upon the hills to the northward. He also sent an officer with a flag of truce into Ventersburg to demand the surrender of the town, and directed Broadwood to detach a regiment and some mounted infantry to occupy it, should the enemy comply. In case they should desire to hold the town the 5-inch guns were brought into position on the captured heights.

Hoping to secure some supplies, particularly bottled beer, before everything should be requisitioned by the army, I rode forward after the flag of truce had gone in and waited where I could see what followed. When, about an hour later, a cavalry force began to advance from the direction of Broadwood upon the town, I knew that all was well, and trotted on to join them. My road led me within a few hundred yards of the town, but, luckily for me, I did not enter it alone, and hurried to join the troops. All of a sudden the ominous patter of rifle shots broke the stillness of the evening, and, turning to where the sound came, I saw a score of Boers standing on the sky-line about a mile away and firing at the advancing cavalry, or, perhaps, for I was much nearer, at me. The next minute there galloped out of the town about a score of Dutchmen, who fled in the direction of their friends on the western sky-line. Had I ridden straight into the town I should have run into these people's jaws. I lost no time in joining the cavalry, and entered the streets with the squadron of Blues. It was a miserable little place, not to be compared with Winburg. There were a few good stores and a small hotel, where I found what I sought; but the whole town was very dirty and squalid. Thirty or forty troopers of Roberts's Horse were firing at the fugitive burghers from the edge of the buildings and gardens, while a score of reckless fellows were galloping after them in excited pursuit. The Boers on the hill kept up a brisk fire to help their comrades in, and not a few of the bullets kicked up the dust in the village streets, without in the least disturbing the women and children who crowded together to look at the war, in blissful ignorance of their danger. When some of these people were told that they would perhaps be killed if they came out of their houses while the fighting was going on, they clutched their children and sought shelter with an energy at which, since, after all, nobody was hurt, it was pardonable to laugh.

Night put an end to all skirmishing, and under its cover the Boers retreated — the greater part to Kroonstadt, which, be it remembered, they meant to hold to the death; but a considerable proportion to the east, where they collected with the commandos under Christiaan de Wet. Broadwood's brigade had captured about a dozen waggons and thirty prisoners. In all there were fifty-two unwounded and seven wounded Boers in our hands at the end of the day. The casualties in Hamilton's force were under fifty. Tucker and Pole-Carew may have lost the same number between them. French, who encountered the most stubborn resistance, had a little over 120. But, in any case, the passage of the Sand River in this long straggling action was cheaply won at a cost of under 250 officers and men.

All our beasts were so exhausted by the labor of dragging the waggons through the steep and rocky drift of the Sand, and by the long pull up the hills on the opposite side, that few of the regiments got their baggage that night, and hence it was impossible to make an early start next morning. But it was known that the Field-Marshal meant to reach Kroonstadt on the next day, and as all the information at our disposal indicated that he Boers were entrenching a strong position along a line of wooded bluffs called the Boschrand, just south of the town, every minute of halt was grudged.

We moved at eleven o'clock, heading direct for Kroonstadt, and persevered for two hours after the sun had set, making in all nearly seventeen miles. The country to our left was flat and open, and as we converged upon the main army we could see, like red clouds with the sunset behind them, the long parallel lines of dust which marked the marches of the Seventh and Eleventh Divisions; and we knew besides that, beyond both columns and west of the railroad, French was driving his weary squadrons forward upon another wide swoop. The army drew together in the expectation of a great action. But for all our marching we could never make up the extra distance we had to cover in coming diagonally from the flank, and as darkness fell we realised that the Seventh Division was drawing across our front, and that Pole-Carew with the guard was striding along ahead of us all. That night Lord Roberts slept at America siding, scarcely six miles from the Boschrand position.

Ian Hamilton marched on again at dawn, transport and convoys struggling along miles behind, and the fine-drawn yet eager infantry close upon the heels of the cavalry screen. At times we listened for the sound of guns, for if the enemy stood, the Field-Marshall must come into contact with them by eight o'clock. And when, after nine o'clock, no cannonade was heard, the rumour ran through the army that the Boers had fled without giving battle, the pace slacked off, and the Infantry began to feel the effects of their exertions.

At eleven a message from Lord Roberts reached General Broadwood to say that it did not matter by which road Hamilton's column marched in, as the enemy was not holding his positions. Thereupon I determined, since there was to be no battle, to see the capture of Kroonstadt, and being mounted on a fresh pony I had bought at Winburg, a beautiful and tireless little beast, by an English blood sire out of a Basuto mare, I soon left the cavalry behind, caught up the rear of Tucker's transport, pushed on four or five miles along the line of march of his division, struck the tail of the Eleventh Division, and finally overtook the head of the Infantry columns about three miles from the town.

Lord Roberts entered Kroonstadt at about mid-day with all his staff. The Eleventh Division, including the Guards' Brigade, marched past him in the market square, and then, passing through the town, went into bivouac on the northern side. The rest of the army halted south of Kroonstadt. Gordon's Cavalry Brigade a mile from the town; the Seventh Division and Ian Hamilton's force three miles away, in a wide valley among the scrub-covered, trench-rimmed hills the Boers had not dared defend. French, whose turning movement had again been obstinately opposed, reached the railway line north of the town too late to intercept any rolling stock. Indeed, Major Hunter-Weston, a daring and enterprising engineer, arrived at the bridge he had hoped to blow up only to find that it had been blown up by the enemy.

Thus, by one long spring from Bloemfontein, Kroonstadt, the new capital of the Free State, was captured. It has the reputation of being one of the prettiest places in the Republic, but even when allowances are made for the circumstances under which we saw it, it does not seem that its fame is just. The town looked a little larger than Winburg, though not nearly so clean and well-kept, and the whole place was smothered in reddish dust, and dried up by the sun. The Boers retreated northward along the railway, in spite of all President Steyn's exhortations, which included the public sjambok-king of several unwilling burghers, and did not stop except to wreck the permanent way until they reached Rhenoster kopjes. The President, with the members of the Executive Council and the seat of Government — which needs to have a good pair of legs beneath it in times like these — withdrew to Lindley, whither, for various reasons, it soon became desirable to follow them.

CHAPTER ELEVEN

LINDLEY

Heilbron: May 22, 1900

Having arrived thus prosperously at Kroonstadt, Lord Roberts determined to halt until his supplies were replenished and the railway line from Bloemfontein in working order. Moreover, in the expectation of a general action outside the town, he had concentrated all his troops and had drawn the Army of the Right Flank close in to the main force. Before he advanced again towards the enemy's position on the Rhenoster River, he wished to extend his front widely, as he had done in the previous operation. The scheme of advance by converging columns required a pause after each concentration before the movement could be repeated; so that while the Field-Marshal himself remained stationary his energetic lieutenant was again on the move.

General Ian Hamilton, with the same troops as before and an addition of four "pom-poms", started from his camp outside Kroonstadt on the 15th, and after a short march encamped on the eastern side of the town preparatory to moving to Lindley, whither President Steyn had withdrawn. The question of supplies was a very troublesome one, and it was no light matter to thrust out fifty miles into hostile country with only three and half days' food and forage in hand. Suppose anything should happen to the convoys which were to follow. Meat in plenty could be found everywhere, but the stores of flour and other farinaceous goods which the farmhouses might contain were insufficient and precarious. Even the benefits of the abundant meat supply were to some extent discounted by the scarcity of wood, for it is not much satisfaction to a soldier to be provided with a leg of mutton if he had no means of cooking. The deficiencies were hardly made good by the arrival of a small convoy, the greater part of which consisted of disinfectants for standing camps, and the rest — so valuable in a grass country — of compressed hay.

Nevertheless, being determined, and trusting, not without reason, in his supply officer, Captain Atcherley, Hamilton started on the 16th, and the infantry bivouacked eighteen miles from Kroonstadt on the Lindley road — it would perhaps be less misleading to write *track*. The cavalry brigade with one corps of mounted infantry under Broadwood were pushed ten miles further on, and seized a fine iron bridge, not marked on any map, which spans an important spruit at Kaalfontein. Here trustworthy information was received that a large force of Boers with guns was retreating before Rundle's column (Eighth Division) northwards upon Lindley, and deeming it important to occupy the town before they arrived, Hamilton ordered the cavalry to hurry on and take possession of the heights to the north of it. It was a double march when ordinary marches were long. The result, however, justified the effort. Broadwood "surprised" — the word is taken from the Boer accounts — Lindley on the 17th. Scarcely fifty Boers were at hand to defend it. A waggon with 60,000l. in specie barely escaped from the clutches of the cavalry. After a brief skirmish the town surrendered. The British loss was three men wounded. Broadwood then retired as directed by his chief to the commanding hill to the north to bivouac. This hill may for convenience be called "Lindley Hill" in the subsequent narrative.

The infantry and baggage also made a long march on the 17th, but as the road was obstructed by several bad spruits or *dongas*, they were still fourteen miles from Lindley when night closed in. Even then the transport was toiling on the road, and a large part of it did not come in, and then in an exhausted condition, until after midnight. I wonder how many people in England realise what a *spruit* is, and how it affects military operations. Those who live in highly developed countries, where the surface of the earth has been shaped to our convenience by the patient labour of many years, are accustomed to find the road running serenely forward across the valleys, and they scarcely notice the bridges and culverts over which it passes. All is different in South Africa. The long column of transport trails across the plain. The veldt in front looks smooth and easy going. Presently, however, there is a block. What is the matter? Let us ride forward and see: and so onward to where the single string of waggons merges in a vast crowd of transport, twenty rows abreast, mule carts, Cape carts, ox waggons, ambulances, and artillery, all waiting impatiently, jostling each other, while drivers and conductors swear and squabble. Here is the spruit — a great chasm in the ground, fifty feet deep, a hundred yards from side to side. The banks are precipitous and impassable at all points except where the narrow single track winds steeply and unevenly down. The bottom is a quagmire, and though the engineers are doing their best to level and improve the roadway, it is still a combination of the Earl's Court water chute and the Slough of Despond. One by one, after a hot dispute for precedence, the waggons advance. The brakes must be screwed up to their tightest grip lest the ponderous vehicles rush forward down the slop and overwhelm their oxen. Even with this precaution the descent of each is a crash, a scramble, and a bump. At the bottom like a feather bed lies the quagmire. Here one waggon in every three sticks. The mules give in after one effort — unworthy hybrids. The oxen strain with greater perseverance. But in the end it is the man who has to do the hauling. Forthwith comes fatigue parties of weary men — it has been a long march already to soldiers fully equipped. Drag ropes are affixed, and so with sweat, blood, and stretching sinew, long whips cracking and whistling, white men heaving and natives yelping encouragement, another waggon comes safely through. And there are seven miles of transport!

On the morning of the 18th the infantry were about to move off, when a pattern of rifle shots to the north of the road reminded us of the presence of the enemy. A foraging party of Major Rimington's Guides had ridden up to a farm, which stood in full view of the camp and flew (or was it hoisted afterwards?) a white flag. Arrived there, they were received by a volley from five Boers in hiding near. Conceive the impudence of these people: five Boers, within a mile of eight thousand British and a powerful cavalry force, fire on a foraging party! Luckily no harm done; cavalry gallop out angrily; Boers vanish among remoter kopjes. "But," said the General, "what about my convoys?"

So it was arranged that Smith-Dorrien should be left where he was (twelve miles west of Lindley) with his own brigade, one battery, and a corps of mounted infantry to help in the expected convoy, and should cut off the corner and rejoin the column at the end of its first march towards Heilbron. Ian Hamilton with the rest of the troops then moved on to Lindley. The march lay through the same class of country hitherto traversed — a pleasant grassy upland which, if not abundantly supplied with water by nature, promised a rich reward to man, should he take the trouble to construct even the simplest irrigation works. Spruits ran in all directions, and only required an ordinary dam, like the *bunds* the peasants build in India, to jewel each valley with a gleaming vivifying lake. The husbanding of water would repair the scarcity of wood, and the tenth year might see the naked grass clothed and adorned with foliage. But at present the country-side is so sparsely populated that the energies of its inhabitants could not produce much effort upon the landscape. The unamiable characteristic of the Boer, to shun the sight of his neighbour's barn, has scattered the farms so widely that little patches of tillage are only here and there to be seen, and the intervening miles lie neglected, often not more than twenty acres of a six thousand acre property being brought into cultivation, which seems rather a pity.

The fair face of the land under its smiling sky was not un-marked by the footprints of war. In the dry weather the careless habits of the soldiers were the constant cause of grass fires. The half-burnt match, tossed idly aside after a pipe was lighted, or an unguarded spark from a cooking fire kindled at once an extensive conflagration. The strong winds drove the devouring blaze swiftly forward across the veldt, clouding the landscape by day with dense fumes of smoke and scarring the scene by night with vivid streaks of flame. So frequent were these grass fires that they became a serious nuisance, wasting in an hour many acres of grazing, proclaiming the movement and marking the track of the army, shifting the marching columns with pungent odours, destroying the field tele-graph, and only extinguished by the heavy dews of the early morn-ing. But in spite of repeated injunctions in the daily orders, the accidents — for which, indeed, there was every excuse — con-tinued, and the plains of brownish grass were everywhere disfig-ured with ugly patches of black ashes which, as the fires burnt outwards, would spread and spread, like stains of blood soaking through khaki.

At length the track, which had been winding among the smooth undulations, rounded an unusually steep hillock of kopje character, and we saw before us at the distance of a mile the pretty little town of Lindley. The cavalry bivouacs covered the nearer slopes of the high hill to the northward. The houses — white walls and blue-grey roofs of iron — were tucked away at the bottom of a regular cup, and partly hidden by the dark green Australian trees. We rode first of all to Broadwood's headquarters, following the ground wire which led thither. Arrived there we learned the news. Boer laagers and Boer patrols had been found scattered about the country to the south-east and north-east. There was occasional firing along the picket line. The town had upon most searching requisition yielded nearly two days' supply, and, most important of all, Piet De Wet, brother of the famous Christiaan, had sent in a message offering to surrender with such of his men as would follow his example, if he were permitted to return to his farm. Broadwood had at once given the required assurance, and Hamilton on his arrival had wired to Lord Roberts fully endorsing the views of his subordinate, and requesting that the agreement might be confirmed. The answer came back with the utmost despatch, and was to the effect that surrender must be unconditional. De Wet, it was remarked, was excluded from the favourable terms of the Proclamation to the Bur-ghers of the Orange Free State, but the fact that he had commanded part of the Republican forces. He could not therefore be permitted to return to his farm. I need not say with what astonishment this decision was received. The messenger carrying the favourable answer was luckily overtaken before he had passed through our picket line and the official letter was substituted. Piet De Wet, who awaited the reply at a farmhouse some ten miles from Lindley, found himself presented with the alternative of continuing the war or going to St. Helena, or perhaps Ceylon; and as events had shown he preferred the former course to our loss in life, honour, and money.

In the afternoon I rode into Lindley to buy various stores in which my waggon was deficient. It is a typical South African town with a large central market square and four or five broad unpaved streets radiating therefrom. There is a small clean-looking hotel, a substantial gaol, a church, and a school-house. But the two largest buildings are the general stores. These places are the depots whence the farmers for many miles around draw all their necessaries and comforts. Owned and kept by Englishmen or Scotchmen, they are built on the most approved style. Each is divided into five or six large well-stocked departments. The variety of their goods is remarkable. You may buy a piano, a kitchen range, a slouch hat, a bottle of hair wash, or a box of sardines over the same counter. The two stores are the rival Whiteley's of the country-side; and the diverse tastes to which they cater prove at once the number of their customers, and the wealth which even the indolent Boer may win easily from his fertile soil.

Personally I sought potatoes, and after patient inquiry I was directed to a man who had by general repute twelve sacks. He was an Englishman, and delighted to see the British bayonets at last. "You can't think," he said, "how we have looked forward to this day."

I asked him whether the Dutch had ill-used him during the war.

"No, not really ill-used us; but when we refused to go out and fight they began commandeering our property, horses and carts at first and latterly food and clothing. Besides, it has been dreadful to have to listen to all their lies and, of course, we had to keep our tongues between our teeth."

It was evident that he hated the Boers among whom his lot had been cast with great earnestness. This instinctive dislike which the British settler so often displays for his Dutch neighbour is a perplexing and not a very hopeful feature of the South African problem. Presently we reached his house (where the potatoes were stored). Above the doorway hung a Union Jack. I said —

"I advise you to take that down."

"Why?" he asked, full of astonishment. "The British are going to keep the country, aren't they?"

"This column is not going to stay here for ever."

"But," with an anxious look, "surely they will leave some soldiers behind to protect us, to hold the town."

I told him I thought it unlikely. Ours was a fighting column. Other troops would come up presently for garrison duty. But there would probably be an interval of at least a week. Little did I foresee the rough fighting which would rage round Lindley for the next three months. He looked very much disconcerted; not altogether without reason.

"It's very hard on us," he said after a pause. "What will happen when the Boers come back? They're just over the hill now."

"That's why I should take the flag down if I were you. If you don't fight, keep your politics till the war is over!" He looked very disappointed, and I think was asking himself how much his enthusiasm had compromised him. After we had settled the potato question to his satisfaction and I had sent the sack away upon my pack pony, he perked up. "Come and see my garden," he said, and nothing loth I went. It was not above a hundred yards square, but its contents proclaimed his energy and the possibilities of the soil. He explained how he had damned a marshy sluit in the side of the hills to the eastward. "Plenty of water at all seasons: this pipe you see, only a question of piping: as much water as ever I want: twenty gardens: grow anything you like, potatoes mostly, cabbages (they were beauties), tomatoes and onions, a vine of sweet white grapes, a bed of strawberries over there — anything: it only wants water, and there's plenty of that if you take the trouble to get it."

The signs of industry impressed me. "How long", I asked, "have you been here?"

"Eight years last February," he replied; "see those trees?"

He pointed to a long row of leafy trees about twenty feet high, which gave a cool shade and whose green colour pleased the eye after looking at so much brown grass. I nodded.

"I planted those myself when I came: they grow quickly, don't they? Only a question of water, and that is only a question of work."

Then I left him and returned to the camp with my potatoes and some information thrown in.

The next morning before breakfast-time there was firing in the picket line south of Lindley. The patter of shots sounded across the valley, and upon the opposite slopes the British patrols could be seen galloping about like agitated ants. I was at the moment with General Hamilton. He watched the distant skirmish from his tent door for a little while in silence. Then he said:

"The scouts and the Kaffirs report laagers of the enemy over there, and over there, and over there" (he pointed to the different quarters). "Now either I must attack them today or they will attack me tomorrow. If I attack them today, I weary my troops; and if I don't we shall have to fight an awkward rear-guard action to get out of this place tomorrow."

He did not say at the time which course he meant to follow, but I felt quite sure he would not take his troops back very far to the south or south-east to chastise impalpable laagers. We were running on schedule time and had to make our connections with the main army, to securing whose smooth and undisturbed march all our efforts must be directed. So I was not surprised when the day passed without any movement on our part.

Very early on the 20th the brigades were astir, and as soon as they light was strong Broadwood's Cavalry began to stream away over the northern ridges. The guns and the greater part of the Infantry followed them without delay, so that by seven o'clock the great column of transport was winding round the corner of Lindley Hill on the road to Heilbron. The fact that parties of the enemy had been observed on all sides except the west, made the operation of disentangling the force from Lindley difficult and dangerous. Broadwood's duty was to clear the way in front. Legge's corps of Mounted Infantry guarded the right flank: and Ian Hamilton himself watched the movement of the rearguard, which consisted of the Derbyshire Regiment, Bainbridge's corps of Mounted Infantry and, as a special precaution, the 82nd Field Battery.

The full light of day had no sooner revealed the march of the troops than the watching Boers began to feel and press the picket line: and an intermittent musketry spread gradually along the whole threequarter circle round Lindley. At eight o'clock our troops evacuated the town itself, at nine, the convey being nearly round Lindley Hill, the pickets commenced to draw in. This was a signal for a decided increase in firing. No sooner were the outposts clear of the town than the Boers in twos and threes galloped into it and began to fire from the houses. All kinds of worthy old gentlemen, moreover, who had received us civilly enough the day before, produced rifles from various hiding-places and shot at us from off their verandahs. Indeed, so quickly did the town revert to the enemy's hands that Somers Somerset, the despatch-rider of *The Times*, was within an ace of being caught. He had arrived late the night before, and having found a comfortable bed at the hotel went to sleep without asking questions. The next thing he remembers is the landlord rushing into his room and crying in great excitement that the Boers were in the town. He scrambled into his clothes and, jumping on his horse, galloped through the streets and was not fired at till he was more than a quarter of a mile away. History does not record whether among such disturbing events he retained his presence of mind sufficiently to settle his hotel bill.

The General and his staff had watched the beginnings of the action from the now deserted camping ground, a dirty waste, littered with rubbish and dotted with the melancholy figures of derelict horses and mules. So soon as the retiring pickets drew north of the town, he mounted and made his way to the top of Lindley Hill. From this commanding table-top the whole scene of action, indeed the whole surrounding country, was visible. At our feet beyond the abandoned bivouac lay the houses of Lindley giving forth a regular rattle of musketry. On either side, east and west, rose two prominent kopjes held by companies of mounted infantry briskly engaged. The tail of the transport serpent was twisting away into safety round the base of our hill. Far away on the broad expanse of down parties of Dutch horsemen cantered swiftly forward; and along a road beyond the eastern kopje rose a steady trickle of mounted men. They moved in true Boer fashion — little independent groups of four or five, now and then a troop of ten or a dozen, here and there a solitary horseman riding back against the general flow. At no particular moment were more than thirty to be seen on the mile of dusty road. Yet to an experienced eye the movement seemed full of dangerous significance. One became conscious of a growing accumulation of force somewhere among the hills to the eastward. The General, who had served on the Indian frontier, understood rearguard actions, and his face was grave, as I had not seen it when larger operations were toward; and at this moment the boom of a heavy gun told us that the advanced troops were also engaged. The Boers knew what they wanted. There was an air of decision about their movements which boded no good to rear or right flank guard. Gallopers were sent off, one to warn the right corps of mounted infantry, another to bid the main body of the force go dead slow, another to the threatened eastern kopje to learn the state of affairs there. The rearguard battery was brought up on to the table-top, and came into action. This was, I think, the key of the situation. The battery planted on Lindley Hill, and casting its shells now in one direction, now in another, compelled the assailants to keep their distance, and helped the pickets into safety and new positions further back. It called to mind some famous knight of history or romance holding an angry rabble back beyond the sweep of his long sword, while his comrades made good their retreat. Under this good protection the pickets, having dutifully held their positions until the convoy was well on its road, scampered in, and the battery itself began to think about retiring. But the trickle of Boers along the eastern roadway had not stopped. Seven or eight hundred men must have passed already; and those that now came galloped as if they had some very tangible objective. "Look out, the right flank!"

But now, the rearguard having disengaged itself from Lindley town, the General's place was with his main body, and we set off to trot and gallop the seven miles that intervened between the head and tail of our force. The firing in front had ceased before we came up. Indeed, the affair had not been of any importance. About seven hundred Boers with three or four guns had obstructed the advance near the Rhenoster River; had even checked the Cavalry screen; Tenth Hussars had two officers wounded; a dozen other casualties in the Brigade; Infantry and guns wanted to clear the way. A Cavalry brigade is not a kopje-smashing machine. "Never mind, here come the cow-guns. Now we shall se." Indeed, as soon as the head of the 21st Brigade began to deploy, the five-inch guns and a field battery opened on the enemy, who thereupon fled incontinently across the river, pursued by the fire of the guns and of the Cavalry "pom-poms".

We were just congratulating ourselves upon the success of these curious operations — curious because the drill books do not con-template both sides fighting rearguard actions at the same time — when half a dozen riderless horses galloped in from somewhere miles away on the right flank. Evidently sharp fighting was pro-ceeding there; the flow of Boers had meant mischief. The peaceful landscape told no tale. No sound of musketry nor sign of action could be distinguished. Indeed, in this scattered warfare one part of a force may easily be destroyed without the rest even knowing that a shot has been fired. "Why scatter them?" asked the armchair strate-gist. "Because if you don't scatter, and haven't got soldiers who are good enough to act when scattered, you will all get destroyed in a lump together."

The General sent directions to the rearguard to communicate with he flank guard; kept another corps of Mounted Infantry handy to support either if necessary, and turned his attention to getting his brigades across the Rhenoster River. While this was proceeding the head of Smith-Dorrien's column, which had marched prosperously from their bivouac near Kaalfontein, came into view, and the Army of the Right Flank stood again united, a fact which suggests some consideration of its functions in the general scheme of Lord Roberts's advance.

After Kroonstadt had been captured the republican forces on the railway retreated to the line of the Rhenoster. Half a mile to the north of the river there rises abruptly from the smooth plain a long line of rocky hills, and in this strong position the Boers had determined to make a stubborn stand. Any force advancing along the railway would indeed have found it a difficult and costly business to cross the river and dislodge an enemy so posted. Other low hills trending away to either flank would have made any turning movement an exceedingly extended and probably a useless operation, for the enemy being on the inside of the circle would have been able to confront the attack wherever it might fall. But the Rhenoster River, as the reader will see by a glance at the map, rises considerably south of the point where it intersects the railway; and so soon as Ian Hamilton's force was across it, the Boers holding the kopjes position were in considerable danger of being cut off. The effect of our crossing the Rhenoster between Lindley and Heilbron should therefore be to clear the march of the main army. All fell out as Lord Roberts had expected; although the Boers had made great preparations to defend Rhenoster, had constructed strong entrenchments and made sidings to detrain their heavy guns, they evacuated the whole position without a shot being fired, compelled by the movement of a column forty miles away to their left flank.

All who understood the scope and cohesion of the operations were delighted at the prospect of getting across the Rhenoster River. The General was determined, rear and flank guard actions notwithstanding, to have his army and transport over that night; and two practicable crossings having been found, infantry, cavalry, guns and baggage began to push across. The last was now increased by the arrival of Smith-Dorrien, who brought with him a much needed convoy with sufficient supplies to carry us on to Heilbron and a march beyond. It was midnight before all the waggons were across; but though this cruel day of march and sun tore the hearts out of the transport animals, and the flocks of sheep were so weary they could scarcely be driven along, we knew that the exertions had not been made in vain.

Late in the evening came the news from the right flank guard. They had waited, fearing to expose the rearguard to a flank attack. The rearguard had made good its retreat. A gap had sprung up between the two bodies. The vigilant Boers had pounced in and stampeded the horses of one mounted infantry company. A sharp, fierce fight followed; rearguard hearing the fusillade swung in to help. Ultimately the Boers were checked sufficiently to enable rear and flank guard to draw inwards together and draw off: but it was by general agreement of participants a very unpleasant affair. The officer commanding the company whose horses were stampeded had particularly interesting experiences. The Boers galloped right in among his men, and a confused scrimmage followed: officer was running towards stampeded horses; on the way he passed a burgher; "Surrender," cried the Dutchman. "No," retorted the officer — an Irishman — (with suitable emphasis) and ran on, whereupon burgher dismounted and began shooting; had four shots and missed every one. Meanwhile officer reached shelter of a convenient rock, turned in just indignation, fitted his Mauser pistol together and fired back. The burgher, finding his enemy behind cover, and himself in the open — by no means the situation for a patriot — jumped on his horse, and would have galloped away but that the officer managed to hit him in the leg with his pistol, and so he dropped, according to the account of an eye-witness, "like a shot rook".

The local advantage, however, rested with the Boers, who hit or captured the greater part of the squadron, including twenty wounded. Concerning these latter, Piet De Wet sent in a flag of truce during the night offering to hand them over if ambulances were sent, and several wounded Boers whom we had taken were given up. This was accordingly done. Our total losses during the 20th were about sixty, some of whom were officers. The Boers admitted a loss of twenty killed and wounded, and it may easily have been more. The army bivouacked on the north bank of the Rhenoster within two marches of the town of Heilbron, upon which it was now designed to move.

CHAPTER TWELVE

CONCERNING A BOER CONVOY

Heilbron: May 22, 1900

Heilbron lies in a deep valley. About it on every side rolls the grassy upland country of the Free State, one smooth grey-green surge beyond another, like the after-swell of a great gale at sea; and here in the trough of the waves, hidden almost entirely from view, is the town itself, white stone houses amid dark trees, all clustering at the foot of a tall church spire. It is a quiet, sleepy little place, with a few good buildings and pretty rose gardens, half-a-dozen large stores, a hotel, and a branch line of its own.

For a few days it had been capital of the Free State. The President, his secretaries, and his councillors arrived one morning from Lindley, bringing the "seat of Government" with them in a Cape cart. For nearly a week Heilbron remained the chief town. Then, as suddenly as it had come, the will-o'-the-wisp dignity departed, and Steyn, secretaries, councills, or Cape cart, hurried away to the eastward, leaving behind them rumours of advancing hosts — and (to this I can testify) three bottles of excellent champagne. That was on Sunday night. The inhabitants watched and wondered all the next day.

On the Tuesday morning, shortly after the sun had risen, Christiaan De Wet appeared with sixty waggons, five guns, and a thousand burghers, very weary, having trekked all night from the direction of Kroonstadt, and glad to find a place of rest and refreshment. "What of the English?" inquired the newcomers, and the Heilbron folk replied that the English were coming, and so was Christmas, and that the country to the southward was all clear for ten miles. Thereat the war-worn commando outspread their oxen and settled themselves to coffee. Forty minutes later the leading patrols of Broadwood's Brigade began to appear on the hills to the south of the town.

Looked at from any point of view, the British force was a formidable array: Household Cavalry, 12th Lancers and 10th Hussars, with P and Q Batteries Royal Horse Artillery (you must mind your P's and Q's with them), two "pom-poms", and two galloping Maxims; and, hurrying up behind them, light horse, mounted infantry, Nineteenth and Twenty-first Brigades, thirty field-guns, more "pom-poms", two great 5-in. ox-drawn siege pieces ("cow guns" as the army calls them), and Ian Hamilton. It was an army formidable to any foe; but to those who now stared upwards from the little town and saw the dark, swift-moving masses on the hills — an avalanche of armed men and destructive engines about to fall on them — terrible beyond words.

"And then," as the poet observes, "there was mounting in hot haste," saddling up of weary ponies, frantic inspanning of hungry oxen cheated of their well-earned rest and feed, cracking of long whips, kicking of frightened Kaffirs; and so pell-mell out of the town and away to the northward hurried the commando of Christiaan De Wet.

The cavalry halted on the hills for a while, the General being desirous of obtaining the formal surrender of Heilbron, and so preventing street-fighting or bombardment. An officer — Lieutenant M. Spender-Clay, of the 2nd Life Guard — was despatched with a flag of truce and a trumpeter; message most urgent, answer to be given within twenty minutes, or Heaven knows what would happen; but all these things take time. Flags of truce (prescribe the customs of war) must approach the enemy's picket line at a walk; a mile and a half at a walk — twenty minutes; add twenty for the answer, ten for the return journey, and nearly half an hour is gone. So we wait impatiently watching the two solitary figures with a white speck above them draw nearer and nearer to the Boer lines; "and", says the brigadier, "bring two guns up and have the ranges taken."

There was just a chance that while all were thus intent on the town, the convoy and commando might have escaped unharmed, for it happened that the northern road runs for some distance eastward along the bottom of the valley, concealed from view. But the clouds of dust betrayed them.

"Hullo! what the deuce is that?" cried an officer.

"What?" said everyone else.

"Why that! Look at the dust. There they go. It's a Boer convoy. Gone away."

And with his halloa the chase began. Never have I seen anything in war so like a fox hunt. At first the scene was uncertain, and the pace was slow with many checks.

Before us rose a long smooth slope of grass, and along the crest the figures of horsemen could be plainly seen. The tail of the waggon train was just disappearing. But who should say how many rifles lined that ridge? Besides, there were several barbed-wire fences, which, as anyone knows, will spoil the best country.

Broadwood began giving all kinds of orders — Household Cavalry to advance slowly in the centre; 12th Lancers to slip forward on the right, skirting the town, and try to look behind the ridge, and with them a battery of horse guns; 10th Hussars, to make a cast to the left, and the rest of the guns to walk forward steadily.

Slowly at first, and silently besides; but soon the hounds gave tongue. Pop, pop, pop — the advanced squadrons — Blues — had found something to fire at, and something that fired back, too; pip-pop, pip-pop came the double reports of the Boer rifles. Bang — the artillery opened on the crest-line with shrapnel, and at the first few shells it was evident that the enemy would not abide the attack. The horsemen vanished over the sky-line.

The leading squadron pushed cautiously forward — every movement at a walk, so far. Infantry brigadiers and others inclined to impatience, ground their teeth, and, thinking there would be no sport that day, went home criticising the master. The leading squadron reached the crest, and we could see them dismount and begin to fire.

We were over the first big fence, and now the scent improved. Beyond the first ridge was another, and behind this, much nearer now, dust clouds high and thick. The General galloped forward himself to the newly-captured position and took a comprehensive view. "Tell the brigade to come here at once — sharp."

A galloper shot away to the rear. Behind arose the rattle of trotting batteries. The excitement grew. Already the patrols were skirting the second ridge. The Boer musketry, fitful for a few minutes, died away. They were abandoning their second position. "Forward, then." And forward we went accordingly at a healthy trot.

In front of the jingling squadrons two little galloping Maxims darted out, and almost before the ridge was ours they were spluttering angrily at the retreating enemy, so that four burghers, as I saw myself, departed amid a perfect hail of bullets, which peppered the ground on all sides.

But now the whole hunt swung northward towards a line of rather ugly-looking heights. Broadwood looked at them sourly. "Four guns to watch those hills, in case they bring artillery against us from them." Scarcely were the words spoken, when there was a flash and a brown blurr on the side of one of the hills, and with a rasping snarl a shell passed overhead and burst among the advancing cavalry. The four guns were on the target without a moment's delay.

The Boer artillerists managed to fire five shots, and then the place grew too hot for them — indeed, after Natal, I may write, even for them. They had to expose themselves a great deal to remove their guns, and the limber and its six horses showed very plainly on the hillside, so that we all hoped to smash a wheel or kill a horse, and thus capture a real prize. But at the critical moment our "pom-poms" disgraced themselves. They knew the range, they saw the target. They fired four shots; the aim was not bad. But four shots — four miserable shots! Just pom-pom, pom-pom. That was all. Whereas, if the Boers had had such a chance, they would have rattled through the whole belt, and sent eighteen or twenty shells in a regular shower. So we all saw with pain how a weapon, which is so terrible in the hands of the enemy, may become feeble and ineffective when used on our side by our own gunners.

After the menace of the Boer artillery was removed from our right flank, the advance became still more rapid. Batteries and squadrons were urged into a gallop. Broadwood himself hurried forward. We topped a final rise.

Then at last we viewed the vermin. There, crawling up the opposite slope, clear cut on a white roadway, was a long line of waggons — ox waggons and mule waggons — and behind everything a small cart drawn by two horses. All were struggling with frantic energy to escape from their pursuers. But in vain.

The batteries spun round and unlimbered. Eager gunners ran forward with ammunition, and some with belts for the "pom-poms". There was a momentary pause while ranges were taken and sights aligned, and then — ! Shell after shell crashed among the convoys. Some exploded on the ground; others, bursting in the air, whipped up the dust all round mules and men. The "pom-poms", roused at last from their apathy by this delicious target and some pointed observations of the General, thudded out strings of little bombs. For a few minutes the waggons persevered manfully. Then one by one they came to a standstill. The drivers fled to the nearest shelter, and the animals strayed off the road or stood quiet in stolid ignorance of their danger.

And now at this culminating moment I must, with all apologies to "Brooksby", change the metaphor, because the end of the chase was scarcely like a fox hunt. The guns had killed the quarry, and the cavalry dashed forward to secure it. It was a fine bag — to wit, fifteen laden waggons and seventeen prisoners. Such was the affair of Heilbron, and it was none the less joyous and exciting because, so far as we could learn, no man on either side was killed, and only one trooper and five horses wounded. Then we turned homewards.

On the way back to the town I found, near a fine farmhouse with deep verandahs and a pretty garden, Boer ambulance waggons, two German doctors, and a dozen bearded men. They inquired the issue of the pursuit; how many prisoners had we taken?

We replied by other questions: "How much longer will the war last?"

"It is not a war any more," said one of the Red Cross men. "The poor devils haven't got a chance against your numbers."

"Nevertheless," interposed another, "they will fight to the end."

I looked towards the last speaker. He was evidently of a different class to the rest.

"Are you", I asked, "connected with the ambulance?"

"No, I am the military chaplain to the Dutch forces."

"And you think the Free State will continue to resist?"

"We will go down fighting. What else is there to do? History and Europe will do us justice."

"It is easy for you to say that, who do not fight; but what of the poor farmers and peasants you have dragged into this war? They do not tell us that they wish to fight. They think they have been made a catspaw for the Transvaal."

"Ah," he rejoined, warmly, "they have no business to say that now. They did not say so before the war. They wanted to fight. It was a solemn pledge. We were bound to help the Transvaalers; what would have happened to us after they were conquered?"

"But, surely you, and men like you, knew the strength of the antagonist you challenged. Why did you urge these simple people to their ruin?"

"We had had enough of English methods here. We knew our independence was threatened. It had to come. We did not deceive them. We told them. I told my flock often that it would not be child's play."

"Didn't you tell them it was hopeless?"

"It was not hopeless," he said. "There were many chances."

"All gone now."

"Not quite all. Besides, chances or no chances, we must go down fighting."

"You preach a strange gospel of peace!"

"And you English," he rejoined, "have strange ideas of liberty."

So we parted, without more words; and I rode my way into the town. Heilbron had one memory of me, and it was one which was now to be revived. In the hotel — a regular country inn — I found various British subjects who had been assisting the Boer ambulances — possibly with rifles. It is not my purpose to discuss the propriety of their conduct. They had been placed in situations which do not come to men in quiet times, and for the rest they were mean-spirited creatures.

While the Republican cause seemed triumphant they had

worked for the Dutch, had doubtless spoken of "damned rooineks", and used other similar phrases; so soon as the Imperial arms predominated they had changed their note; had refused to go on commando in any capacity, proclaiming the Britons never should be slaves, and dared the crumbling organism of Federal government to do its worst.

We talked about the fighting in Natal which they had seen from the other side. The Action Homes affair cropped up. You will remember that we of the irregular brigade plumed ourselves immensely on this ambuscading of the Boers — the one undoubted score we ever made against them on the Tugela.

"Yes," purred my renegades, "you caught the damned Dutchmen fairly then. We were delighted, but of course we dared not show it." (Pause.) "That was where De Mentz was killed."

De Mentz! The name recalled a vivid scene — the old field cornet lying forward, grey and grim, in a pool of blood and a litter of empty cartridge cases, with his wife's letter clasped firmly in his stiffening fingers. He had "gone down fighting"; had had no doubts what course to steer. I knew when I saw his face that he had thought the whole thing out. Now they told me that there had been no man in all Heilbron more bitterly intent on the war, and that his letter in the *Volsstem*, calling on the Afrikanders to drive the English scum form the land, had produced a deep impression.

"Let them", thus it ran, "bring 50,000 men, or 80,000 men, or even" — it was a wild possibility — "100.000, yet we will overcome them." But they brought more than 200,000, so all his calculations were disproved, and he himself was killed with the responsibility on his shoulders of leading his men into an ambush which, with ordinary precautions, might have been avoided. Such are war's revenges. His widow, a very poor woman, lived next door to the hotel, nursing her son who had been shot through the lungs during the same action. Let us hope he will recover, for he had a gallant sire.

CHAPTER THIRTEEN

ACTION OF JOHANNESBURG

Johannesburg: June 1, 1900

On the 24th of May, Ian Hamilton's force, marching west from Heilbron, struck the railway and joined Lord Roberts's main column. The long marches, unbroken by a day's rest, the short rations to which the troops had been restricted, and the increasing exhaustion of horses and transport animals seemed to demand a halt. But a more imperious voice cried "Forward!" and at daylight the travel-strained brigades set forth, boots worn to tatters, gun horses dying at the wheel, and convoys struggling after in vain pursuit — "Forward to the Vaal."

And now the Army of the Right Flank became the Army of the Left; for Hamilton was directed to move across the railway line and march on the drift of the river near Boschbank. Thus, for the first time it was possible to see the greater part of the invading force at once.

French, indeed, was already at Parys, but the Seventh and Eleventh Divisions, the Lancer Brigade, the corps troops, the heavy artillery, and Hamilton's four brigades were all spread about the spacious plain, and made a strange picture; long brown columns of infantry, black squares of batteries, sprays of cavalry flung out far to the front and flanks, 30,000 fighting men together, behind them interminable streams of waggons, and, in their midst, like a pillar of cloud that led the hosts of Israel, the war balloon, full blown, on its travelling car.

We crossed the Vaal on the 26th prosperously and peacefully. Broadwood, with his cavalry, had secured the passage during the previous night, and the Infantry arriving found the opposite slopes in British hands. Moreover, the engineers, under the indefatigable Boileau, assisted by the strong arms of the Blues and Life Guards, had cut a fine broad road up and down the steep river banks.

Once across we looked again for the halt. Twenty-four hours' rest meant convoys with full rations and forage for the horses. But in main army crossing at Vereeniging, demoralisation of the enemy increasing, only one span of the railway bridge blown up, perhaps Johannesburg within three days — at any rate, "try", never mind the strain of nerve and muscle or the scarcity of food.

Forward again. That day Hamilton marched his men eighteen

miles — ("ten miles", say the text-books on war, "is a good march for a division with baggage", and our force, carrying its own supplies, had ten times the baggage of a European division!) — and succeeded besides in dragging his weary transport with him. By good fortune the cavalry discovered a little forage — small stacks of curious fluffy grass called manna, and certainly heaven-sent — on which the horses subsisted and did not actually starve. All day the soldiers pressed on, and the sun was low before the bivouac was reached. Nothing untoward disturbed the march, and only a splutter of musketry along the western flank guard relieved its dullness.

At first, after we had crossed the Vaal, the surface of the country was smooth and grassy, like the Orange River Colony, but as the column advanced northwards the ground became broken — at once more dangerous and more picturesque. Dim blue hills rose up on the horizon, the rolling swells of pasture grew sharper and less even, patches of wood or scrub interrupted the level lines of the plain, and polished rocks of conglomerate or auriferous quarts showed through the grass, like the bones beneath the skin of the cavalry horses. We were approaching the Rand.

On the evening of the 27th, Hamilton's advance guard came in touch with French, who, with one mounted infantry and two cavalry brigades, was moving echeloned forward on our left in the same relation to us as were we to the main army.

The information about the enemy was that, encouraged by the defensive promise of the ground, he was holding a strong position either on the Klip Riviersberg, or along the line of the gold mines crowning the main Rand reef. On the 28th, in expectation of an action next day, Hamilton made but a short march. French, on the other hand, pushed on to reconnoitre, and if possible — for the cavalry were very ambitious — to pierce the lines that lay ahead.

I rode with General Broadwood, whose brigade covered the advance of Hamilton's column. The troops had now entered a region of hills which on every side threatened the march and limited the view.

At nine o'clock we reached a regular pass between two steep rocky ridges. Form the summit of one of these ridges a wide landscape was revealed. Northwards across our path lay the black line of the Klip Riviersberg, stretching to the east as far as I could see, and presenting everywhere formidable positions to the advancing force. To the west these frowning features fell away in more grassy slopes, from among which, its approach obstructed by several rugged under-features, rose the long smooth ridge of the Witwatersrand reef. The numerous grass fires which attend the march of any army in dry weather — the results of our carelessness, or, perhaps, of the enemy's design — veiled the whole prospect with smoke, and made the air glitter and deceive like the mirages in the Soudan. But one thing showed with sufficient distinctness to attract and astonish all eyes. The whole crest of the Rand ridge was fringed with factory chimneys. We had marched nearly 500 miles through a country which, though full of promise, seemed to European eyes desolate and wild, and now we turned a corner suddenly, and there before us sprang the evidence of wealth, manufacture, and bustling civilisation. I might have been looking from a distance at Oldham.

The impression was destroyed by the booming of shotted guns, unheard, by God's grace, these many years in peaceful Lancashire. French was at work. The haze and the distance prevented us from watching too closely the operations of the cavalry. The dark patches of British horsemen and the white smoke of the Dutch artillery were the beginning and the end of our observations. But, even so, it was easy to see that French was not making much progress

As the afternoon wore on the loud reverberations of heavy cannon told that the Boers had disclosed their real position, and we knew that something more substantial than cavalry would be required to drive them from it. In the evening French's brigades were seen to be retiring across the Klip River, and the night closed in amid the rapid drumming of the Vickers-Maxims covering his movement, bringing with it the certainty of an Infantry action on the morrow.

At twelve o'clock a despatch from the Cavalry Division reached Hamilton. French's messenger said that he cavalry were having a hot fight and were confronted by several 40-pounder guns, but the stout-hearted commander himself merely acquainted Hamilton with his orders from headquarters, to march *via* Florida to Driefontein, and made no allusion to his fortunes nor asked for assistance. Indeed, as we found out later, his operations on the 28th had been practically confined to an artillery duel, in which, though the expenditure of ammunition was very great and the noise alarming, the casualties — one officer and eight men — were fortunately small.

But the Boers, seeing the cavalry retire at dusk, claimed that they had repulsed the first attack; their confidence in the strength of the Rand position was increased; their resistance on the next day was consequently more stubborn; and the *Standard and Diggers' News* was enabled to terminate a long career of exaggeration and falsehood by describing one more "blood British defeat with appalling slaughter."

The event of the next day admitted of no such misinterpretation.

The orders from headquarters for the 29th were such as to involve certain fighting should the enemy stand. French, with the Cavalry Division, was to march around Johannesburg to Driefontein; Ian Hamilton was directed on Florida; the main army, under the Field-Marshall, would occupy Germiston and seize the junctions of the Natal, Cape Colony, and Potchefstroom lines. These movements, which the chief had indicated by flags on the map, were now to be executed — so far as possible — by soldiers on the actual field.

The operations of the main army are not my concern in this letter; but it is necessary to state the result, lest the reader fail to grasp the general idea, and, while studying the detail, forget their scale and meaning.

Advancing with great speed and suddenness through Elandsfontein, Lord Roberts surprised the Boers in Germiston, and after a brief skirmish drove them in disorder from the town, which he then occupied. So precipitate was the flight of the enemy, or so rapid the British advance, that nine locomotives and much other rolling stock were captured, and the line from Germiston southward to Vereeniging was found to be undamaged. The importance of these advantages on the success of the operations can scarcely be overestimated. The problem of supply was at one modified, and though the troops still suffered privations from scarcity of food the anxieties of their commanders as to the immediate future were removed.

French had camped for the night south of the Klip River, just out of cannon shot of the enemy's position, and at eight o'clock on the morning of the 29th he moved off westward, intending to try to penetrate, or, better till, circumvent, the barrier that lay before him.

Such ground as he had won on the previous day he held with mounted infantry, and thus masking the enemy's front he attempted to pierce if he could not turn his right. For these purposes the force at his disposal — three horse batteries, four "pom-poms", and about 3,000 mounted men — was inadequate and unsuited. But he knew that Ian Hamilton, with siege guns, field guns, and two infantry brigades, was close behind him, and on this he reckoned.

Firing began about seven o'clock, when the Boers attacked the Mounted Infantry Corps holding the positions captured on the 28th, and who were practically covering the flank movement of the rest of the Cavalry Division and the march of Hamilton's column. The mounted infantry, who were very weak, were gradually compelled to fall back, being at one time enfiladed by two Vickers-Maxims and heavily pressed in front.

But their resistance was sufficiently prolonged to secure the transference of force lines from right to left. By ten o'clock French had gone far enough west to please him, and passing round the edge of a deep swamp turned the heads of his regiments sharply to their right (north), and moved towards the Rand ridge and its under features.

By the vigorous use of his horse artillery he cleared several of the advanced kopjes, and had made nearly two miles progress north of the drainage line of the Klip River, when he was abruptly checked. A squadron sent forward against a low fringe of rocks, clumping up at the end of a long grass glacis, encountered a sudden burst of musketry fire, and returned, pursued by shell, with the information that mounted men could work no further northwards.

Meanwhile Hamilton, who had determined to lay his line of march across the Doornkop ridges (of inglorious memory), and whose infantry, baggage, and guns were spread all along the flat plain south of the Klip, was drawing near. French halted his brigades and awaited him. The instructions from headquarters defined very carefully the relations which were to be observed between the two generals. They were to co-operate, yet their commands were entirely separate. Should they attack the same hill at once, French, as a lieutenant-general and long senior to Hamilton, would automatically assume command. But this contingency was not likely to arise from the military situation, and the good feeling and mutual confidence which existed between these two able soldiers, and which had already produced golden results at Elandslaagte, made the possibility of any misunderstanding still more remote.

French was joined by Hamilton at one o'clock, and they discussed the situation together. French explained the difficulty of further direct advance. He must move still more to the west. On the other hand, Hamilton, whose force was eating its last day's rations, could make no longer detour, and must break through there and then — frontal attack, if necessary. So all fitted in happily. The Cavalry Division moved to the left to co-operate with the infantry attack by threatening the Boer right, and, in order that this pressure might be effective, Hamilton lent Broadwood's Brigade and two corps of mounted infantry to French for the day. He himself prepared to attack what stood before him with his whole remaining force.

By two o'clock the cavalry in brown swarms had disappeared to the westward, both infantry brigades were massed under cover on the approaches of the Rand ridge, and the transport of the army lay accumulated in a vast pool near the passage of the Klip — here only a swamp, but further east a river. The artillery duel of the morning had died away. The firing on the right, where the mounted infantry still maintained themselves, was intermittent. The reconnaissance was over. The action was about to begin, and in the interval there was a short, quiet lull — the calm before the storm. The soldiers munched their biscuits silently under the sun blaze. The officers and staff ate a frugal luncheon. Ian Hamilton with his aide-de-camp, the Duke of Marlborough, shared the contents of my wallets. I watched the General closely. He knew better than the sanguine people who declared the Boers had run away already. No one understood better than he what a terrible foe is the rock-sheltered Mauser-armed Dutchman. In spite of its cavalry turning movement, and other embellishments, the impending attack must be practically frontal. Supply did not allow a wider circle: to stop was to starve; and the position before us — half-a-dozen clusters of rock, breaking from the smooth grass upward slopes, except in colour, like foam on the crests of waves, natural parapet and glacis combined, and, beyond all, the long bare ridge of the Rand lined with who should say what entrenchments or how many defenders — a prospect which filled all men who knew with the most solemn thoughts.

For my part, having seen the infantry come reeling back in blood ruin two or three times from such a place and such a foe, though I risked no repute on the event — scarcely my life — I confess to a beating heart. But the man who bore all the responsibility, and to whom the result meant everything, appeared utterly unmoved. Indeed, I could almost imagine myself the General and the General the Press Correspondent, though perhaps this arrangement would scarcely have worked so well.

At three o'clock precisely the Infantry advanced to the attack. Major-General Bruce-Hamilton directed the left attack with the Twenty-first Brigade, and Colonel Spens the right with the Nineteenth Brigade. The whole division was commanded by General Smith-Dorrien. The lateness of the hour gave scarcely any time for the artillery preparation, and the artillery came into action only a few minutes before the infantry were exposed to fire.

It must be noticed that the combination of the batteries and the support which they afforded to the attack were scarcely so effective as might have been expected from the number of guns available. But the General commanding a mixed force is bound to trust the various specialists under him, at least until experience has shown them to be deficient in energy or ability.

The infantry advance was developed on the most modern principles. Each brigade occupied a front of more than a mile and three-quarters, and the files of the first line of skirmishers were extended no less than thirty paces. Bruce-Hamilton, with the left attack, started a little earlier than the right brigade, and, with the City Imperial Volunteers in the fire line, soon had his whole command extended on the open grass.

A few minutes after three, French's guns were heard on the extreme left, and about the same time the firing on the right swelled

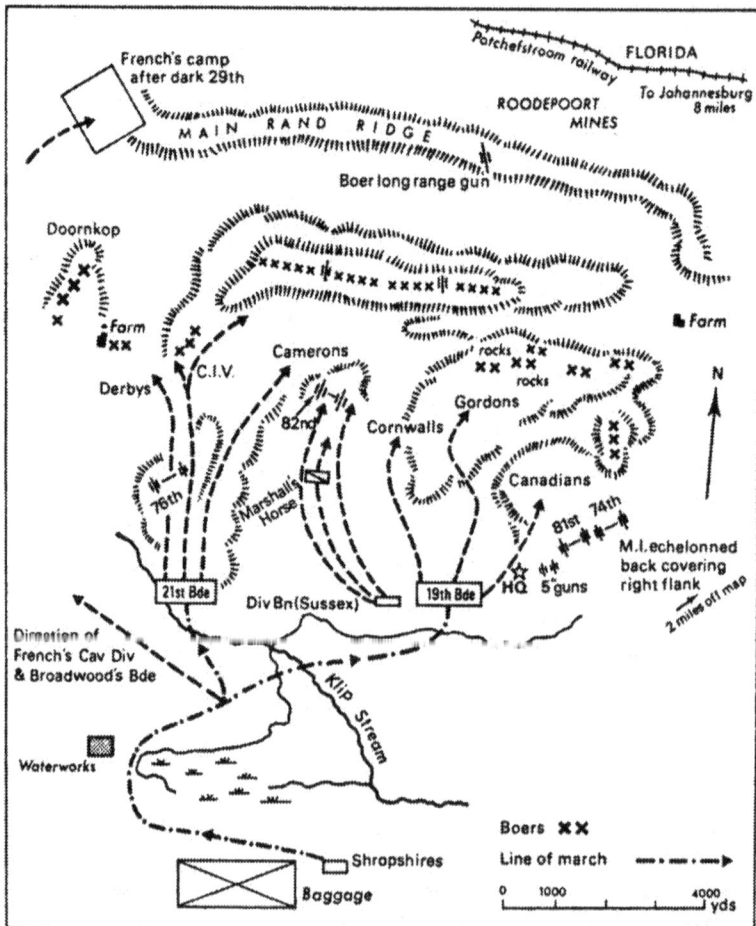

IAN HAMILTON'S ACTION BEFORE JOHANNESBURG

up again, so that by the half-hour the action was general along the whole front of battle — an extent of a little over six miles.

The left attack, pressed with vigour, and directed with skill by General Bruce-Hamilton, led along a low spur, and was designed to be a kind of inside turning movement to assist the right in conformity with the cavalry action now in full swing. The City Imperial Volunteers moved forward with great dash and spirit, and in spite of a worrying fire from their left rear, which increased in proportion as they moved inwards towards the right, drove the Boers from position after position. While there is no doubt that French's pressure beyond them materially assisted their advance, the rapid progress of this Twenty-first Brigade entitled them and their leader to the highest credit. The Cameron Highlanders and the Sherwood Foresters supported the attack. The Boers resisted well with artillery, and their shells caused several casualties among the advancing lines; but it was on the right that the fighting was most severe.

The leading battalion of the Nineteenth Brigade chanced — for there was no selection — to be the Gordon Highlanders; nor was it without a thrill that I watched this famous regiment move against the enemy. Their extension and advance were conducted with machine-line regularity. The officers explained what was required to the men. They were to advance rapidly until under rifle fire, and then to push on or not as they might be instructed.

With impassive unconcern the veterans of Chitral, Dargai, and Bara Valley, Magersfontein, Paardeberg, and Houtnek walked leisurely forward, and the only comment recorded was the observation of a private: "Bill, this looks like being a kopje day." Gradually the whole battalion drew out clear of the covering ridge, and long dotted lines of brown figures filled the plain. At this moment two batteries and the two 5-in. guns opened from the right of the line, and what with the artillery of French and Bruce-Hamilton there was soon a loud cannonade.

The Dutch replied at once with three or four guns, one of which seemed a very heavy piece of ordnance on the main Rand ridge, and another fired from the kopje against which the Gordons were marching. But the Boer riflemen, crouching among the rocks, reserved their fire for a near target. While the troops were thus approaching the enemy's position, the two brigades began unconsciously to draw apart. Colonel Spens's battalions had extended further to the right that either Ian Hamilton or Smith-Dorrien had intended. Bruce-Hamilton, pressing forward on the left, found himself more and more tempted to face the harassing attack on this left rear. Both these tendencies had to be corrected. The Gordons were deflected to their left by an officer, Captain Higginson, who galloped most pluckily into the firing line in spite of a hail of bullets. Bruce-Hamilton was ordered to bear in to his right and disregard the growing pressure behind his left shoulder. Nevertheless a wide gap remained. But by mischance Ian Hamilton contrived to profit. Smith-Dorrien had already directed the only remaining battalion — the Sussex — to fill up the interval, and the General-in-Chief now thrust a battery forward through the gap, almost flush with the skirmish line of the Infantry on its left and right.

The fire of these guns, combined with the increasing pressure from the turning movements both of Bruce-Hamilton and French, who was now working very far forward in the west, weakened the enemy's position on the kopje which the Gordons were attacking. Yet when every allowance has been made for skilful direction and bold leading, the honours, equally with the cost of the victory, belong more to the Gordon Highlanders than to all the other troops put together.

The rocks against which they advanced proved in the event to be the very heart of the enemy's position. The grass in front of them was burnt and burning, and against this dark background the khaki figures showed distinctly. The Dutch held their fire until the attack was within 800 yards, and then, louder than the cannonade, the ominous rattle of concentrated rifle fire burst forth. The black slope was spotted thickly with grey puffs of dust where the bullets struck as with advancing soldiers, and tiny figures falling by the way told of heavy loss. But the advance neither checked nor quickened.

With remorseless stride, undisturbed by peril or enthusiasm, the Gordons swept steadily onward, changed direction half left to avoid, as far as possible, an enfilade fire, changed again to the right to effect a lodgment on the end of the ridge most suitable to attack, and at last rose up together to charge. The black slope twinkled like jet with the unexpected glitter of bayonets. The rugged sky-line bristled with kilted figures, as, in perfect discipline and disdainful silence, those splendid soldiers closed on their foe.

The Boers shrank from the contact. Discharging their magazines furiously, and firing their guns twice at point-blank range, they fled in confusion to the main ridge, and the issue of the action was no longer undecided.

Still the fight continued. Along the whole infantry front a tremendous rifle fire blazed. Far away to the left French's artillery pursued the retreating Boers with shells. The advanced batteries of Hamilton's force fired incessantly. The action did not cease with the daylight. The long line of burning grass cast a strange, baleful glare on the field, and by this light the stubborn adversaries maintained their debate for nearly an hour.

At length, however, the cannonade slackened and ceased, and the rifles soon imitated the merciful example of the guns. The chill and silence of the night succeeded the hot tumult of the day. Regiments assembled and reformed their ranks, ambulances and baggage waggons crowded forward from the rear, the burning veldt was beaten out, and hundreds of cooking fires gleamed with more kindly meaning through the darkness.

The General rode forward, to find the Gordons massed among the rocks they had won. The gallant Burney, who commanded the firing line, was severely wounded. St. John Meyrick was killed. Nine officers and eighty-eight soldiers had fallen in the attack; but those that remained were proud and happy in the knowledge that they had added to the many feats of arms which adorn the annals of the regiment — one that was at least the equal of Elandslaagte or Dargai; and, besides all this, they may have reflected that by their devotion they had carried forward the British cause a long stride to victory, and, better than victory, to honourable peace. Ian Hamilton spoke a few brief words of thanks and praise to them — "the regiment my father commanded and I was born in" — and told them that in a few hours all Scotland would ring with the tale of their deeds. And well Scotland may, for no men of any race could have shown more soldier-like behaviour.

Then we rode back to our bivouac, while the lanterns of searching parties moved hither and thither among the rocks, and voices cried "Bearer party this way!" "Are there any more wounded here?" with occasional feeble responses.

Owing to the skilful conduct of the attack, the losses, except among the Gordons, were not severe — in all about 150 killed and wounded. The result of the fight — the action of Johannesburg, as we called it — was the general retreat of all the enemy west of the town under Delarey and Viljoen northwards toward Pretoria, and in conjunction with the Field-Marshal's movements, the surrender of the whole of the Witwatersrand.

French, continuing his march at dawn to Driefontein, captured one gun and several prisoners. Ian Hamilton entered Florida, and found there and at Maraisburg sufficient stores to enable him to subsist until his convoys arrived.

CHAPTER FOURTEEN

THE FALL OF JOHANNESBURG

Johannesburg: June 2

Morning broke and the army arose ready, if necessary, to renew the fight. But the enemy had fled. The main Rand ridge still stretched across our path. Its defenders had abandoned all their positions under the cover of darkness. Already French's squadrons were climbing the slopes to the eastward and pricking their horses forward to Elandsfontein (North). So Hamilton's force, having but six miles to march to Florida, did not hurry its departure, and we had leisure to examine the scene of yesterday's engagement. Riding by daylight over the ground of the Gordon's attack, we were still more impressed by the difficulties they had overcome. From where I had watched the action the Boers had seemed to be holding a long black kopje, some forty feet high, which rose abruptly from the grass plain. It had turned out that the aspect of steepness was produced by the foreshortening effects of the burnt grass areas; that in reality the ground scarcely rose at all, and that what we had thought was the enemy's position was only a stony outcrop separated from the real line of defence by a bare space of about 200 yards.

Looking around I found a Highlander, a broad-shouldered, kind-faced man, with the Frontier ribbon, which means on a Gordon tunic much hard fighting; and judging with reason that he would know something of war, I asked him to explain the ground and its effect.

"Well, you see, sir," he said, in quick-spoken phrases, "we was regularly tricked. We began to lose men so soon as we got on the burnt grass. Then we made our charge up to this first line of little rocks, thinking the Boers were there. Of course they weren't here at all, but back over there, where you see those big rocks. We were all out of breath, and in no order whatever, so we had to sit tight here and wait."

"Heavy fire?" I asked. He cocked his head like an expert.

"I've seen heavier; but there was enough. We dropped more than forty men here. 'Tis here poor Mr.____ was wounded; just behind this stone. You can see the blood here yet, sir — this mud's it."

I looked as required, and he proceeded:

"We knew we was for it then; it didn't look like getting on, and we couldn't get back — never a man would ha' lived to cross the black ground again with the fire what it was, and no attack to fright them off their aim. There was such a noise of the bullets striking the rocks that the officers couldn't make themselves heard, and such confusion too! But two or three of them managed to get together after a while, and they told us what they wanted done . . . and then, of course, it was done all right."

"What was done? What did you do?"

"Why, go on, sir, and take that other line — the big rocks — soon as we'd got our breath. It had to be done."

He did not seem the least impressed with his feat of arms. He regarded it as a piece of hard work he had been set to do, and which — this as a matter of course — he had done accordingly. What an intrepid conquering machine to depend on in the hour of need! — machine and much more, for this was a proud and intelligent man, who had thought deeply upon the craft of war, and had learnt many things in a severe school.

I had not ridden a hundred yards further, my mind full of admiration for him and his type, when a melancholy spectacle broke upon the view. Near a clump of rocks eighteen Gordon Highlanders — men as good as the one I had just talked with — lay dead in a row. Their faces were covered with blankets, but their grey stockinged feet — for the boots had been removed — looked very pitiful. There they lay stiff and cold on the surface of the great Banket Reef. I knew how much more precious their lives had been to their countrymen than all the gold mines the lying foreigners say this war was fought to win. And yet, in view of the dead and the ground they lay one, neither I nor the officer who rode with me could control an emotion of illogical anger, and we scowled at the tall chimneys of the Rand.

General Ian Hamilton, General Smith-Dorrien, all their staffs, and everyone who wished to pay a last tribute of respect to brave men, attended the funerals. The veteran regiment stood around the grave, forming three sides of a hollow square — Generals and staff filled the other. The mourning party rested on their arms, reversed; the Chaplain read the Burial Service, the bodies were lowered into the trench, and the pipes began the lament. The wild, barbaric music filled the air, stirring the soldier, hitherto quite unmoved, with a strange and very apparent force. Sad and mournful was the dirge wailing of battles ended, of friendships broken, and ambitions lost; and yet there were mingled with its sadness many notes of triumph, and through all its mourning rang the cry of hope.

The whole of Hamilton's force had marched by ten o'clock, but even before that hour the advanced guard had passed through Florida and picketed the hills beyond. Florida is the Kew Gardens of Johannesburg. A well-built dam across a broad valley has formed a deep and beautiful lake. Carefully planted woods of Australian pines offer a welcome shade on every side. The black and white pointed chimneys of the mine buildings rise conspicuous above the dark foliage. There is a small but comfortable hotel, called "The Retreat", to which on Sundays, in times of peace, the weary speculations whose minds were shattered by the fluctuations of the Exchange were wont to resort for rest of diversion. Everywhere along the reef the signs of industry and commerce were to be seen. Good macadamised roads crossed each other in all directions; flashy advertisements caught the eye. A network of telegraphs and telephones ran overhead. The ground was accurately marked out with little obelisks of stone into "Deeps" and "Concessions", and labelled with all the queer names which fill the market columns of the newspapers. In a word, it seemed — to us dirty, tattered wanderers — that we had dropped out of Africa and War, and come safely back to Peace and Civilisation.

Since the soldiers had eaten their last day's rations, and the only food they had had that morning came form any odds and ends the regiment might have saved, it was imperative to find some supplies. The Field-Marshal had ordered that no troops should enter Johannesburg until he should specially direct; but, finding little to eat in Florida, Hamilton sent his supply officers and a squadron as far as Maraisburg; whence they presently returned with a quantity of tinned rabbit and sardines, and with the news that the Boers were said to be occupying a position near Langlaagte mine.

During the morning we caught a train and some prisoners. The train was returning from Potchefstroom, guarded by six armed burghers, and on rifles being pointed, it stopped obediently and surrendered. The other prisoners were brought in by the cavalry and mounted infantry, who had caught them wandering about without their horses. Among them was Commandant Botha — not Louis or Phillip — but Botha of the Zoutspansberg commando, a brave and honest fellow, who had fought all through the war from Talana Hill until the last action; but who was quite content that Fate had decided he should fight no more. Hearing of him under guard, and near headquarters, I went to see him. He displayed no bitterness whatever, and seemed quite prepared to accept the decision of war. He inquired anxiously whether he would be sent to St. Helena, and evinced a childish horror of the sea. While we were chatting, one of the other Boer prisoners, who had been looking hard at us, said, suddenly, in very good English.

"The last time I saw you, you were in my position and I in yours."

He then went on to tell me that he had been in the commando that destroyed the armoured train. "I felt very sorry for you that day," he said.

I remarked that it was much worse to be taken prisoner at the beginning of a war than near the end, as he was.

"Do you think this is the end?" asked the Commandant quickly.

"I should ask you that."

"No, no — not yet the end. They will fight a little more. Perhaps they will defend Pretoria — perhaps you will have to go to Lydenburg; but it will not be very long now."

And then, since both he and his companion had been through the Natal campaign, we fell to discussing the various actions. Ian Hamilton came up while we were talking. I had just told the Commandant that we considered the Boers had made a fatal strategic mistake in throwing their main strength into Natal, instead of merely holding the passes, masking Mafeking and Kimberley, and marching south into the colony with every man and gun they could scrape together. He admitted that perhaps that might be so; "but," said he, "our great mistake in Natal was not assaulting Ladysmith — the Platrand position, you know — the day after our victory at Lombard's Kop. We blame Joubert for that. Many of us wanted to go on them. There were no fortifications; the soldiers were demoralised. If once we had taken Platrand (Cæsar's Camp) you could not have held the town. How many men had you on top of it?"

"Only a picket for the first week," said the General.

"Ah! I knew we could have done it. What would have happened then?"

"We should have had to turn you out."

The Commandant smiled a superior smile. The General continued: "Yes — with the bayonet — at night; or else, as you say, the town could not have been held."

"Presently," said Botha, "you pulled yourselves together, but for three days after Nicholson's Nek there was no fear of bayonets. If we had stormed you then — (then we had all our men and no Buller to think about) — you would not have been able to turn us out."

Hamilton reflected. "Perhaps not," he said, after a pause. "Why didn't Joubert try it?"

"Too old," said Botha, with complete disdain; "you must have young men for fighting."

That was, so far as I remember, the end of the conversation; but, a fortnight later, I met Botha a free man in the streets of Pretoria. He told me he had been released on parole, so that evidently his frank manliness had not been lost upon the General.

After lunch I became very anxious to go into, and, if possible, through Johannesburg. An important action had been fought, witnessed by only two or three correspondents; and since the enemy lay between the force and the telegraph wire no news could have been sent home. Hamilton, indeed, had sent off two of Rimington's Guides early in the morning with despatches; but they were to make a wide sweep to the south, and it was not likely, if they got through at all, that they would reach Lord Roberts until late. The shortest, perhaps the safest, road lay through Johannesburg itself. But was the venture worth the risk? While I was revolving the matter in my mind on the verandah of the temporary headquarters, there arrived two cyclists from the direction of the town. I got into conversation with one of them, a Frenchman, Monsieur Lautré by name. He had come from the Langlaagte mine, with which undertaking he was connected. There were no Boers there, according to him. There might or might not be Boers in the town. Could a stranger get through? Certainly, he thought, unless he were stopped and questioned. He undertook there and then to be my guide if I wished to go; and it being of considerable importance to get the telegrams through to London, I decided, after a good many misgivings, to accept his offer. The General, who wanted to send a more detailed account of his action, and to report his arrival at Florida, was glad to avail himself even of this precarious channel. So the matter was immediately settled. Lautré's friend, a most accommodating person, got off his bicycle without demur and placed it at my disposal. I doffed my khaki and put on a suit of plain clothes which I had in my valise, and exchanged my slouch hat for a soft cap. Lautré put the despatches in his pocket, and we started without much ado.

The tracks were bad, winding up and down hill, and frequently deep in sand; but the machine was a good one, and we made fair progress. Lautré, who knew every inch of the ground, avoided all highways, and led me by devious paths from one mine to another, around huge heaps of tailings, across little private tram lines, through thick copses of fir trees, or between vast sheds of machinery, now silent and idle. In three-quarters of an hour we reached Langlaagte, and here we found one of Rimington's scouts pushing cautiously forward towards the town. We held a brief parley with him, behind a house, for he was armed and in uniform. He was very doubtful of the situation ahead; only knew for certain that the troops had not yet entered Johannesburg. "But," said he, "the Correspondent of *The Times* passed me more than two hours ago."

"Riding?" I asked.

"Yes," he said, "a horse."

"Ah," said my Frenchman, "that is no good. He will not get through on a horse. They will arrest him." And then, being quite fired with the adventure: "Besides, we will beat him, even if, unhappily, he escapes the Boers."

So we hurried on. The road now ran for the most part downhill, and the houses became more numerous. The day was nearly done and the sun drew close to the horizon, throwing out long shadows on the white track before us. At length we turned into a regular street.

"If they stop us," said my guide, "speak French. *Les Français sont en bonne odeur ici.* You speak French, eh?"

I thought my accent might be good enough to deceive a Dutchman, so I said yes; and thereafter our conversation was conducted in French.

We avoided the main thoroughfares, bicycling steadily on through the poorer quarters. Johannesburg stretched about me on every side, silent, almost deserted. Groups of mood-looking people chatted at the street corners, and eyed us suspiciously. All the shops were shut. Most of the houses had their windows boarded up. The night was falling swiftly, and its shades intensified the gloom which seemed to hang over the town, on this the last day of its Republican existence.

Suddenly, as we crossed a side lane, I saw in the street parallel to that we followed three mounted men with slouch hats, bandoliers, and that peculiar irregular appearance which I have learned to associate with Boers. But to stop or turn back was now fatal. After all, with the enemy at their gates, they had probably concerns of their own to occupy them. We skimmed along unhindered into the central square, and my companion, whose coolness was admirable, pointed me out the post-office and other public buildings, speaking all the time in French. The slope now rose against us so steeply that we dismounted to push our machines. While thus circumstanced I was alarmed to hear the noise of an approaching horse behind me. With an effort I controlled my impulse to look back.

"*Encore un Boer,*" said Lautré lightly. I was speechless. The man drew nearer, overtook and pulled his horse into a walk beside us. I could not help — perhaps it was the natural, and, if so, the wise, thing to do — having a look at him. He was a Boer sure enough, and

I think he must have been a foreigner. He was armed *cap-à-pié*. The horse he rode carried a full campaigning kit on an English military saddle. Wallets, saddle-bags, drinking-cup, holsters — all were there. His rifle was slung across his back, he wore two full bandoliers over his shoulders and a third round his waist — evidently a dangerous customer. I looked at his face and our eyes met. The light was dim, or he might have seen me change colour. He had a pale, almost ghastly visage, peering ill-favoured and cruel from beneath a slouch hat with a large white feather. Then he turned away carelessly. After all, I suppose he thought it natural a poor devil of a townsman should wish to look at so fine a cavalier of fortune. Presently he set spurs to his horse and cantered on. I breathed again freely. Lautré laughed.

"There are plenty of cyclists in Johannesburg," he said. "We do not look extraordinary. No one will stop us."

We now began to approach the south eastern outskirts of the town. If the original scheme of advance had been carried out, Lord Roberts's leading brigade should be close at hand. Lautré said, "Shall we inquire?" But I thought it better to wait. As we progressed the streets became still more deserted, and at last we found ourselves quite alone. For more than half a mile I did not see a single person. Then we met a shabby-looking man, and now, no one else being in sight, the night dark, and the man old and feeble, we decided to ask him.

"The English," he said with a grin, "why, their sentinels are just at the top of the hill."

"How far?"

"Five minutes — even less."

Two hundred yards further on three British soldiers came in sight. They were quite unarmed, and walking casually forward into the town. I stopped them and asked what brigade they belonged to. They replied Maxwell's.

"Where is the picket line?"

"We haven't seen no pickets," said one of them.

"What are you doing?"

"Looking for something to eat. We've had enough of 'arf rations."

I said, "You'll get taken prisoners or shot if you go on into the town."

"Wot's that, guvnor?" said one of them, deeply interested in this extraordinary possibility.

I repeated, and added that the Boers were still riding about the streets.

"Well, then, I ain't for it," he said with decision. "Let's go back and try some of them 'ouses near the camp."

So we all proceeded together.

I discovered no picket line at the edge of the town. Maxwell must have had one somewhere, but it certainly did not prevent anyone from passing freely; for we were never challenged, and, walking on, soon found ourselves in the middle of a large bivouac. I now became of some use to my companion, for if he knew the roads I knew the army. I soon found some officers of my acquaintance, and from them we learned that Lord Roberts's headquarters were not at Elandsfontein (South), but back at Germiston, nearly seven miles away. It was now pitch dark, and all signs of a road had vanished; but Lautré declared he knew his way, and, in any case, the messages — press and official — had to go through.

We left the camp of Maxwell's Brigade and struck across country in order to cut into the main southern road. A bicycle now became a great encumbrance, as the paths wound through dense fir woods, obstructed by frequent wire fences, ditches, holes, and high grass. Lautré, however, persisted that all was well, and, as it turned out, he was right. After about an hour of this slow progress we reached the railway, and, seeing more camp fires away to the left, turned along it. Half a mile in this direction brought us to another bivouac, which we likewise entered unchallenged. I asked a soldier whose brigade he belonged to, but he did not know, which was painfully stupid of him. A group of officers were gathered round an enormous fire a few yards away, and we went up to them to ask. Chance had led me to General Tucker's mess. I had know the commander of the Seventh Division in India, when he was stationed at Secunderabad, and he welcomed me with his usual breezy courtesy. He had been sent off with his leading brigade late in the afternoon to try to join hands with French, and so complete the circle round Johannesburg; but darkness had curtailed his march. Besides this, no communications having yet come through from the cavalry, he was uncertain where French was. Naturally he was interested to hear what had passed on the west of the town, and about the stirring action of the previous day. From him I got some whisky and water, and clear directions to the Field-Marshal's headquarters. They were, it appeared, two mile beyond Germiston, a mile and a half west of the road, in a solitary house on a small hill which stood beyond a large tank. And in case these indications might have been of little avail in the dark, he led us a few feet up the slope, and there we saw that, on the blackness of the night, flamed a regular oblong of glittering lights. It was the camp of the Eleventh Division. Somewhere near that were the Chief's headquarters. Thus instructed, we resumed our journey.

Another half-hour of walking brought us, as Lautré had promised, to a good firm road, and the bicycles quickly made amends for their previous uselessness. The air was cold, and we were glad to spin along at a fair ten miles an hour. At this rate twenty minutes brought us into Germiston. Not knowing where I should be likely to find dinner, or a bed, I dismounted opposite the hotel, and, seeing lights and signs of occupation, went inside. Here I found Mr. Lionel James, the principal Correspondent of *The Times*. I asked him if his subordinate had arrived from Hamilton's force. He said, "No"; and when I told him he had started two hours in front of me, looked much concerned; whereat the Frenchman could not conceal a heartless grimace. I offered to give him some account of the action for his own use (for what is more detestable than a jealous journalist?), but he said that I had had the good luck to come through, and that he would not think of depriving me of my advantage. Alas! the days of newspaper enterprise in war are over. What can one do with a censor, a forty-eight hours' delay, and a fifty-word limit on the wire? Besides, who can complete with Lord Roberts as a special correspondent? None against the interest of his daily messages; very few against their style and simple grace. Never mind. It is all for the best.

We dined hastily and not too well, secured the reservation of half the billiard table, should all other couches fail, and set out again this time tired and footsore. After two miles of dusty track the camp was reached. I found more officers who knew where Army Headquarters were. We sent the despatches in by an orderly, and after a few minutes Lord Kerry came out and said that the Chief wanted to see the messengers.

Now, for the first time in this war, I found myself face to face with our illustrious leader. The room was small and meanly furnished, and he and his staff, who had just finished dinner, sat round a large table which occupied the greater part of the floor. With him were Sir William Nicholson (who arranges all the transport of the army, a work the credit of which is given to Lord Kitchener) and Colonel Neville Chamberlayne, his private secretary, both of them soldiers of the practical Indian school, where you have real fighting, both of them serving once more under their commander of Afghan days. There, too, was Sir Henry Rawlinson, whom I had last seen round Sir George White's table, the night Dundonald broke into Ladysmith; and Sir James Hills-Johnes, who won the Victoria Cross in the Indian Mutiny, and aides-de-camp and others whom I cannot remember.

The Field-Marshal rose from his place, shook hands, and bade us, in most ceremonious fashion, to be seated. He had read half of Hamilton's despatch.

"The first part of this," he said, "we knew already. Two guides — Rimington's, I think — got in here about an hour ago. They had a dangerous ride, and were chased a long way, but escaped safely. I am glad to hear Hamilton is at Florida. How did you get through?"

I told him briefly. His eyes twinkled. I have never seen a man before with such extraordinary eyes. I remember to have been stuck with them on several occasions. The face remains perfectly motionless, but the eyes convey the strongest emotions. Sometimes they blaze with anger, and you see hot yellow fire behind them. Then it is best to speak up straight and clear, and make an end quickly. At others there is a steel grey glitter — quite cold and uncompromising — which has a most sobering effect on anyone who sees it. But now the eyes twinkled brightly with pleasure or amusement or approbation, or, at any rate, something friendly.

"Tell me about the action," he said.

So I told him all I knew, much as it is set down in these pages, though not nearly at such length; but I don't think the tale lost in the telling. From time to time he asked questions about the Artillery concentration, or the length of front of the Infantry attack, and other technical matters, on which I was luckily well-informed. The fact that the troops had no rations seemed to disturb him very much. He was particularly interested to hear of Hamilton's novel attack "at thirty paces extension"; of the manner in which the batteries had been rammed almost into the firing line; but most of all he wanted to hear about the Gordons' charge. When I had done he said: "The Gordons always do well." Then he asked what we proposed to do. Lautré said he would go back forthwith; but the Chief said, "Much better stay here for the night; we will find you beds"; so of course we stayed. He asked me whether I meant to go back next morning. I said that as I had got my messages to the telegraph office I thought, upon the whole, that I would not run any more risks, but wait and see the British occupation of the town. He laughed at this, and said that I was quite right, and would be very ill-advised to be caught again. Then he said that he would send a letter to Hamilton in the morning, bade us all "good-night", and retired to his waggon. I, too, found a comfortable bed- — he first for a month — and being thoroughly worn out soon fell asleep.

Part of Lord Roberts's letter that he wrote to Ian Hamilton next day was published in the orders of the flanking column. In some ways it explains why the private solider will march further for "Bobs Bahadur" than for anyone else in the world.

"I am delighted at your repeated successes, and grieve beyond measure for your poor fellows being without their proper rations. A trainful shall go to you to-day. I expect to get the notice that Johannesburg surrenders this morning, and we shall then march into the town. I wish your column, which has done so much to gain possession of it, could be with us.

"Tell the Gordons that I am proud to think I have a Highlander as one of the supporters on my coat-of-arms."

CHAPTER FIFTEEN

THE CAPTURE OF PRETORIA

Pretoria: June 8, 1900

The Commander-in-Chief had good reasons — how good we little knew — for wishing to push on at once to the enemy's capital, without waiting at Johannesburg. But the fatigue of the troops and the necessities of supply imposed a two days' halt. On the 3rd of June the advance was resumed. The army marched in three columns. The left, thrown forward in echelon, consisted of the Cavalry Division under French; the centre was formed by Ian Hamilton's force; and the right or main column nearest the railway comprised the Seventh and Eleventh Divisions (less one brigade left to hold Johannesburg), Gordon's Cavalry Brigade, and the Corps Troops all under the personal command of the Field Marshal.

The long forward stride of the 3rd was, except for a small action against French, unchecked or unopposed by the Boers, and all the information which the Intelligence Department could collect seemed to promise a bloodless entry into the capital. So strong was the evidence that at dawn on the 4th of June Hamilton's column was diverted from its prescribed line of march on Elandsfontein[2] and drawn in towards the man army, with orders to bivouac on Pretoria Green, west of the town. French, whom the change of orders did not reach, pursued his wide turning movement, and encountered further opposition in a bad country for cavalry.

At ten o'clock it was reported that Colonel Henry, with the corps of mounted infantry in advance of the main column, was actually in the suburbs of Pretoria without opposition. The force continued to converge, and Ian Hamilton had almost joined Lord Roberts's force when the booming of guns warned us that our anticipations were too sanguine. The army had just crossed a difficult spruit, and Colonel Henry with the mounted infantry had obtained a lodgment on the heights beyond. But here they were sharply checked. The Boers, apparently in some force, were holding a wooded ridge and several high hills along the general line of the southern Pretoria forts.

---

2   Yet another Elandsfontein, situated to the west of Pretoria.

Determined to hold what he had obtained, Lord Roberts thrust his artillery well forward, and ordered Ian Hamilton to support Colonel Henry immediately with all mounted troops. This was speedily done. The horsemen galloped forward, and, scrambling up the steep hillsides, reinforced the thin firing line along the ridge. The artillery of the Seventh Division came into action in front of the British centre. The Boers replied with a brisk rifle fire, which reached all three batteries, and drew from them a very vigorous cannonade.

Meanwhile the infantry deployment was proceeding. The 14th Brigade extended for attack. Half an hour later Pole-Carew's batteries prolonged the line of guns to the right, and about half past two the corps and heavy artillery opened in further prolongation. By three o'clock fifty guns were in action in front of the main army, and both the Seventh and Eleventh Divisions had assumed preparatory formations. The balloon ascended and remained hanging in the air for an hour — a storm signal.

During this time Hamilton was pushing swiftly forward, and Smith-Dorrien's 19th Infantry Brigade occupied the line of heights, and thus set free the mounted troops for a turning movement. The 21st Brigade supported. The heights were so steep in front of Hamilton that his artillery could not come into action, and only one gun and one "pom-pom" could, by great exertion, be dragged and man-handled into position. The fire of these pieces, however, caught the Boers holding the wooded ridge in enfilade, and was by no means ineffective.

So soon as Hamilton had collected the mounted troops he sent them to reinforce Broadwood, whom he directed to move round the enemy's right flank. The ground favored the movement, and by half past four the cavalry were seen debouching into the plain beyond the Boer position, enveloping their flank and compromising their retreat.

Colonel de Lisle's corps of mounted infantry, composed mainly of Australians, made a much shorter circuit, and reaching the level ground before the cavalry espied a Boer Maxim retreating towards the town. To this they immediately gave chase, and the strong Waler horses were urged to their utmost speed. The appearance of this clattering swarm of horsemen must have been formidable to those below. But we who watched from the heights saw what Ian Hamilton, who was in high spirits, described as "a charge of infuriated mice" streaming across the brown veldt; so great are the distances in modern war.

Towards four o'clock the cannonade all along the front had

died away, and only the heavy artillery on the right of Pole-Carew's Division continued to fire, shelling the forts, whose profile showed plainly on the sky-line, and even hurling their projectiles right over the hills into Pretoria itself. So heavy had the artillery been that the Boers did not endure, and alarmed as well by the flank movement they retreated in haste through the town; so that before dusk their whole position was occupied by the Infantry without much loss. Night, which falls at this season and in this part of the world as early as half past five, then shut down on the scene, and the action — in which practically the whole Army Corps had been engaged — ended.

The fact that the forts had not replied to the British batteries showed that their guns had been removed, and that the Boers had no serious intention of defending their capital. The Field-Marshal's orders for the morrow were, therefore, that the army should advance at daybreak on Pretoria, which it was believed would then be formally surrendered. Meanwhile, however, Colonel de Lisle, with the infuriated mice — in other words, the Australians — was pressing hotly on, and at about six o'clock, having captured the flying Maxim, he seized a position within rifle shot of the town. From here he could see the Boers galloping in disorder through the streets, and, encouraged by the confusion that apparently prevailed, he sent an officer under flag of truce to demand the surrender. This the panic-stricken civil authorities, with the consent of Commandant Botha, obeyed, and though no British troops entered the town until the next day, Pretoria actually fell before midnight on the 4th of June.

As soon as the light allowed the army moved forward. The Guards were directed on the railway station. Ian Hamilton's force swept round the western side. Wishing to enter among the first of the victorious troops the town I had crept away from as a fugitive six months before, I hurried forward, and, with the Duke of Marlborough, soon overtook General Pole-Carew, who, with his staff, was advancing towards the railway station. We passed through a narrow cleft in the southern wall of mountains, and Pretoria lay before us — a picturesque little town with red or blue roofs peeping out among masses of trees, and here and there an occasional spire of factory chimney. Behind us, on the hills we had taken, the brown forts were crowded with British soldiers. Scarcely two hundred yards away stood the railway station.

Arrived at this point, General Pole-Carew was compelled to wait to let his Infantry catch him up; and while we were delayed a locomotive whistle sounded loudly, and, to our astonishment — for had not the town surrendered? — a train drawn by two engines steamed out of the station on the Delagoa Bay line. For a moment we stared at this insolent breach of the customs of war, and a dozen staff officers, aides-de-camp, and orderlies (no mounted troops being at hand) started off at a furious gallop in the hoped of compelling the train to stop, or at least of shooting the engine-driver, and so sending it to its destruction. But wire fences and the gardens of the houses impeded the pursuers, and, in spite of all their efforts, the train escaped, carrying with it ten trucks of horses, which might have been very useful, and one truck-load of Hollanders. Three engines with steam up and several trains, however, remained in the station, and the leading company of Grenadiers, doubling forward, captured them and their occupants. These Boers attempted to resist the troops with pistols, but surrendered after two volleys had been fired, no more, fortunately, being hurt in the scrimmage.

After a further delay, the Guards, fixing bayonets, began to enter the town, marching through the main street, which was crowded with people, towards the central square, and posting sentries and pickets as they went. We were naturally very anxious to know what had befallen our comrades held prisoners all these long months. Rumour said they had been recovered during the night to Waterfall Boven, 200 miles down the Delagoa Bay line. But nothing definite was known.

The Duke of Marlborough, however, found a mounted Dutchman who said he knew where all the officers were confined, and who undertook to guide us, and without waiting for the troops, who were advancing with all due precautions, we set off at a gallop.

The distance was scarcely three-quarters of a mile, and in a few minutes, turning a corner and crossing a little brook, we saw before us a long tin building surrounded by a dense wire entanglement. Seeing this, and knowing its meaning too well, I raised my hat and cheered. The cry was instantly answered from within. What followed resembled the end of an Adelphi melodrama.

The Duke of Marlborough called on the commandant to surrender forthwith. The prisoners rushed out of the house into the yard, some in uniform, some in flannels, hatless or coatless, but all violently excited. The sentries threw down their rifles. The gates were flung open, and while the rest of the guards — they numbered fifty-two in all — stood uncertain what to do, the long-penned-up officers surrounded them and seized their weapons. Someone — Grimshaw of the Dublin Fusiliers — produced a Union Jack (made during imprisonment out of a Vierkleur). The Transvaal emblem was torn down, and, amid wild cheers, the British flag was hoisted over Pretoria. Time 8.47, June 5.

The commandant then made a formal surrender to the Duke of Marlborough of 129 officers and 39 soldiers whom he had in his custody as prisoners of war, and surrendered, besides himself, 4 corporals and 48 Dutchmen. These latter were at once confined within the wire cage, and guarded by their late prisoners; but, since they had treated the captives well, they have now been permitted to take the oath of neutrality and return to their homes. The anxieties which the prisoners had suffered during the last few hours of their confinement were terrible, nor did I wonder, when I heard the account, why their faces were so white and their manner so excited. But the reader shall learn the tale from one of their number, nor will I anticipate.

At two o'clock Lord Roberts, the staff, and the foreign attachés entered the town, and proceeded to the central square, wherein the Town Hall, the Parliament House, and other public buildings are situated. The British flag was hoisted over the Parliament House amid some cheers. The victorious army then began to parade past it, Pole-Carew's Division, with the Guards leading, coming from the south, and Ian Hamilton's force from the west. For three hours the broad river of steel and khaki flowed unceasingly, and the townfolk gazed in awe and wonder at those majestic soldiers, whose discipline neither perils nor hardships had disturbed, whose relentless march no obstacles could prevent.

With such pomp and the rolling of drums the new order of things was ushered in. The former Government had ended without dignity. One thought to find the President — stolid old Dutchman — seated on his stoep reading his Bible and smoking a sullen pipe. But he chose a different course. On the Friday preceding the British occupation he left the capital and withdrew along the Delagoa Bay Railway, taking with him a million pounds in gold, and leaving behind him a crowd of officials clamouring for pay, and far from satisfied with the worthless cheques they had received, and Mrs. Kruger, concerning whose health the British people need not further concern themselves.

I cannot end this letter without recalling for one moment the grave risks Lord Roberts bravely faced in order to strike the decisive blow and seize Pretoria. When he decided to advance from Vereeniging without waiting for more supplies, and so profit by the enemy's disorder, he played for a great stake. He won, and it is very easy now to forget the adverse chances. But the facts stand out in glaring outline: that if the Boers had defended Pretoria with their forts and guns they could have checked us for several weeks; and if, while we were trying to push our investment, the line had been cut behind us, as it has since been cut, nothing would have remained but starvation or an immediate retreat on Johannesburg, perhaps on the Vaal. Even now our position is not thoroughly secure, and the difficulties of subjugating a vast country, though sparsely populated, are such that the troops in South Africa are scarcely sufficient. But the question of supplies is for the present solved. The stores of Johannesburg, and still more of Pretoria, will feed the army for something over a fortnight, and in the meanwhile we can re-open our communications, and perhaps do much more. But what a lucky nation we are to have found, at a time of sore need and trouble, a General great enough to take all risks and overcome all dangers.

CHAPTER SIXTEEN

"HELD BY THE ENEMY"

Extracts from the journal of Lieutenant H. Frankland,
Royal Dublin Fusiliers, lately prisoner of war at Pretoria.

L ieutenant Frankland was captured by the Boers when the armoured train was destroyed at Chieveley, in Natal, on the 15th
of November, 1899. He was carried as a prisoner to Pretoria, where
he arrived on the 19th of November, and where he remained until
the 5th of June, 1900, when Pretoria fell and the greater part of the
prisoners were set free by their victorious comrades.

*   *   *

"*November 19th.* — To wake up and find oneself enclosed in the
space of a few acres for an indefinite period is scarcely pleasant;
however, one cannot always be miserable. The monotony will, I
have no doubt, become very trying, but for the first few days I have a
good deal to do. The State Model School, which has been turned
into a prison for the officers, is a building of rectangular shape. A
long corridor runs through the centre, and on both sides of this are
the rooms, where the officers sleep. They are supplied with a spring
bed and two blankets apiece, while the whole place is lighted by
electricity. At one end is the dining-room and gymnasium.

"In front is the road, from which the building is separated by
iron railings. Behind there is a sort of back garden where the police
and soldier servants live in tents, and where the kitchen and the
bathroom are situated. This piece of ground is surrounded on three
sides by a six-foot fence of corrugated iron, and the whole place is
watched by a cordon of armed police, about fifteen being on duty
always. The Government here generously supplies the officers with
bread and water, half a pound of bully beef a day, and groceries. We
have a small piece of ground and a gymnasium for exercise. As there
are, alas! about fifty officers here, we have formed a sort of mess,
and for the sum of three shillings a day we improve our scanty
allowance of food. They have supplied us with a suit of clothes each,
but mine was much too big for me. I began to write my diary this
evening, and had a long talk with Garvice in my regiment, who told
me how he had been captured. Dinner 7.30; bed, and sleep.

"*November 20th.* — It looks as if the rest of my diary for several
months would contain each day the words, 'the same as usual'. I

have only been here forty-eight hours, but the monotony has already begun to show itself. Not the monotony only, but the want of freedom, the want of news, the knowledge that the rest of the war will be carried out without my share in its victories, when, had it not been for some unhappy fate, I might yet have seen many an action — all these combine to oppress and irritate my mind. I tried to make a sketch of the armoured train, but it was not a success, and I must begin again tomorrow. The very length of empty time in front of me makes me quite patient.

"*November* 21*st*. — It is getting extremely hot. The lack of open space to walk in makes me feel lazy, and one gets quite tired after going a few times around the building. What one most looks forward to are the meals, and these are not very satisfying. But of course I am still suffering from the appetite of freedom, and I have no doubt that a month or so of this sort of life will make me feel less ravenous. I wrote some in my diary, and commenced another sketch of the armoured train, which I hope to be able to send to the *Graphic*. Churchill has written asking to be released, but he does not expect any result. The mosquitoes here are very troublesome, and I have been constantly bitten.

"*November* 23*rd*. — The mail was supposed to go to-day, so I found occupation in a few letters. It is still very sultry. I succeeded in getting through a good deal of my diary, and, after writing nearly all day, played a game of rounders in the evening. This last occupation appears to cause much annoyance to the police, who frequently get hit by the ball. Another game here is fives, which we play with a tennis ball in the gymnasium. There seems to be some news about, but we can get nothing out of these people. By these people I mean Malan — a spiteful, objectionable animal — who ought to be at the front, were he not a coward; Opperman, a slightly more agreeable person, of large dimensions, and Dr. Gunning, a much more amiable fellow. It seems absurd that they do not allow us to buy papers. What harm could we do with them?

"Some of the restrictions are so childish, and tend to make life here so sickening, that I am sure if curses could harm the Transvaal Government it would not be long-lived.

"This morning Churchill was visited by De Souza, the Secretary of War, by the Under-Secretary for Foreign Affairs, and others, and there followed a very animated discussion about the causes and the justice of the war. It was a drawn game, and they all talked at once at the end, especially Churchill. I am afraid for his sake he is not likely to be exchanged or released. The Boers have got to hear of the part he played in the armoured train episode.

"*November 24th*. — Evidently we have won a victory at Belmont; its results are immediately apparent here. They have suddenly become much more lenient and complacent. We are actually allowed newspapers, and the President is considering the question of beer. The papers admit that the British drove the Free Staters from their position at Belmont, but with a great loss, while that of the Boers is practically *nil*. Rumours say that General Joubert is cut off between Estcourt and Mooi River; how I hope it is true!

"*November 26th*. — The Rev. Mr. Hofmeyr is a prisoner here, and held service this morning, when he delivered a most eloquent address. There is a harmonium in one of the rooms, and Mr. Hofmeyr, who sings very well, gives us some very good music. He knows a lot of old English songs, which are pleasant to hear, although the rather suggest the Psalm beginning 'By the waters of Babylon'. Hofmeyr, though a Dutchman, is an ardent supporter of the Imperial cause, and he has in consequence been very cruelly treated by the Boers before he came here.

"It is quite touching to see how the Boers try to hide their defeat. All the accounts are cooked, but even De Souza acknowledges that if things go on as at present the war will soon be over. There have been several days' fighting south of Kimberley, and Buller is advancing steadily. On the Natal side Joubert passed Estcourt, and reached Mooi River, where he was attacked by the new division and defeated. In retiring he was attacked by part of the Estcourt garrison, result unknown. He will probably retire on Colenso.

"*November 27th*. — Not much news today. According to the *Volksstem* British lost fifteen hundred at Belmont, and the Boers nine killed and forty wounded. However, they can't deny that the Free Staters were licked, and De Souza admits that Kimberley will probably be relieved shortly. Moreover, Khama is said to have risen. This has disturbed them all exceedingly, and Opperman is highly indignant.

"*November 30th*. — I find nothing to record here except the scraps of news one gets in the newspapers, all else is monotonous — appalling monotony. In the evening one feels it most, and sometimes I don't think I can endure it for another month. All sorts of absurd rumours are spread about here by that intelligent paper the *Volksstem*. The latest is that four British regiments have refused to fight, being in sympathy with the Republican cause. I wonder whether Buller will desert to the Boer side? The fact remains that the papers give no news whilst there must be plenty, and this looks as if the untold news must be bad for them. We hear that General

Forestier-Walker has been killed, and that Lord Methuen is seriously wounded. This morning the rumour runs that our troops have occupied Colenso. The regiment is sure to be there. How I wish I were with it!

"*December 4ᵗʰ.* — No real news, but various and contradictory rumours. The Boers have begun to acknowledge their losses, and the papers have long lists of killed and wounded. Major ___, of the West Yorks, arrived today, having been captured near Estcourt. From him I learned that all was well there. A few days ago three battalions — West Yorks, Bordereres and Second Queen's — went out and attacked the Boers. Apparently the engagement was indecisive, and the losses on either side not very great. The rumour goes that Buller is in Natal, and not in the Free State after all. Of course he is advancing to the relief of Ladysmith. We all think that his plan will be to hold the Boers in front at Colenso while he takes a large force around by the flank. The Boers have retired beyond the river, and have blown up the Tugela railway bridge. On the other side, Lord Methuen's Division is having severe fighting; he has defeated the Boers at Modder River, and the relief of Kimberley is imminent. The papers do not publish much news themselves, but occasionally publish some of the English cuttings with sarcastic editorial comments. In the Dutch version of the *Volksstem* they slate the Free Staters unmercifully for having run away at Modder River.

"Oh, that we might be exchanged. Joubert has wired *via* Buller to England advocating such a step.

"*December 15ᵗʰ.* — '*Tempus fugit*', and it has not been quite so dull as usual. First, and most important of all, Churchill has escaped. Whether he has made it good or not is still uncertain; but he has now been gone two days, and I have great hopes. Besides the excitement there has been a very amusing side to the affair. Of course Churchill was the very last person who ought to have gone. He was always talking and arguing with the officials, and was therefore well known, and, indeed, scarcely a day passes without Dr. Gunning or Mr. De Souza inquiring for him. His plans for escape were primitive; but, being still in prison, I must not write anything about this part of the affair. Let it suffice that Churchill got away without any trace left behind. Next morning, as it chanced, it was the day for the barber to come and have him, and having only just woke up I put the barber off rather feebly by saying that Churchill had gone to the bath-room, and would not need shaving. What should the detective who accompanied the barber do but wait outside the bath-room, and, finding no Churchill, began to suspect. Gunning then came upon the scene, closely followed by Opperman, both asking and seeking anxiously for their captive. Their distress at finding him gone was really pathetic. They immediately put on all kinds of restrictions. No papers, calling rolls, not allowing anyone into the yard outside the building after 8 p.m., and stopping all beer. I am reminded of the fable 'Le Corbeau et le Renard', which ends, *'Le Corbeau . . . jura, mais un peu tard, qu'on ne l'y prendroit plus'*. Curiously enough, the day after Churchill had escaped an order is said to have come from General Joubert for his release. However, I have no doubt but that this was all made up to excuse themselves for not being able to catch him. I do hope he gets away.

"Our spirits are constantly on the rise and fall. At one time we are about to be exchanged, at another nothing has been heard of it; at one time there is a brilliant British success, greatly, modified, of course, by the enlightened *Volksstem* editor, at another a crushing British defeat, with all the Generals and thousands of soldiers killed and wounded. Yesterday we heard of a splendid achievement of the British troops in Ladysmith in smashing up the 84-pounder at Lombard's Kop, several Howitzers and a Maxim. Then came the defeat of General Gatacre at Stormberg, and the capture of 600 prisoners, and on the top of this the victory which the Boers claim at Magersfontein. All this is very terrible. I think I feel almost as miserable as I did the night I was captured. Are the British troops ever going to drive the Boers back? Will they ever come and take Pretoria? or will they, on the other hand, like in '81, and — no, impossible — and yet who will dare predict? It is too awful to hear all these shocking reports, and to be able to do nothing oneself. One always imagines on these occasions one's presence at the scene of fighting absolutely indispensable if there is to be a victory. However, these miserable days cannot last for ever. Perhaps they are even now at an end. De Souza, with a faltering voice, has confessed that Buller is advancing at last in great force. He must win.

"*December* 23rd. — No more news. The authorities are getting more and more silly and disagreeable; all kinds of babyish restrictions are invented to annoy us. Churchill has got to Delagoa Bay, and has wired his safe arrival to De Souza. Hurrah!

*   *   *

"I have not dared until now, when all is a failure, to set down in this book any account of the one occupation that has prevented us from going mad with disappointment in these sad times. About the middle of the month Haldane devised a plan of making a tunnel from under our room across the road. The five fellows in our dormitory and Le Mesurier, who shifted his abode for the purpose, began about ten days ago. First, we thought of cutting a hole in the floor, but, on looking round, we suddenly found a trap-door already made. Beneath the floor there is a curious place. The rafters are supported by stone walls, so that underneath there is a series of compartments about twenty-four feet by four, with access from one to another by means of man-holes in each wall. We commenced digging in the compartment next to the one under the trap-door. The ground at first was very hard, but with chisels and implements taken from the gymnasium, we managed to get down four feet of the shaft in about four days. It was a queer sight to see two half-naked figures digging by candle light, for we used to work in reliefs of two — one to dig and the other to cast away the earth in boxes or jugs. Suddenly, one day, we broke through the hard crust and came to some soft clay soil. We were delighted at this, and expected to get through it in now time; but, alas! with the soft earth came water, and without pumps, bale as we would, we could not get rid of it. Every morning the shaft was completely bilged; so, having dug down six feet, our plan was brought to an end, and we had to screw up our trap-door again in bitter disappointment. The officers of the Gloucester Regiment are digging too, but they are sure to find the same difficulties.

"*Christmas Day, 1899.* — I can scarcely realise that it is Christmas, the day I have hitherto spent at home with family and friends. I can see the rooms decorated with holly and 'Merry Christmas' cut in white paper and pasted on red Turkish twill hanging over the doorway. A Merry Christmas! What irony! The time, of course, was bound to come when the circle at home would be broken; but little did I dream when or under what unhappy circumstances. A Merry Christmas! to a prisoner — not when his countrymen, victorious and full of enthusiasm, are marching rapidly to his release, but when the armies of his country, beaten back, lie far away; when, helpless himself, despair seizes his heart; when reverses grow into disasters and the might of the dear old land in which he trusted ooomo to havo woakonod and diod. A Happy Chriotmaol with tho New Year black, uncertain, and unknown. Of course we drank the health of the Queen at dinner — in lime-juice. 'Twas all we had; but we meant it none the less.

"*December 30th.* — They say there was only 1,200 casualties at Colenso; but we have just heard that ___ and ___ of our regiment have been killed. O God! it seems too awful. To hear of all one's friends crippled or dead; all the best are picked off, and here are we tied up quite safely with our beastly skins unhurt, and not likely to run the slightest danger while our comrades are losing their lives. We must win this war.

"*January* 1st. — I have had many arguments as to whether this is the commencement of a new century or not, and after much reasoning I have decided that as it is the year 1900, or the nineteen hundredth year, it is the last of the nineteenth century and not the beginning of the twentieth. Whatever it may be, this is a hateful place to spend the beginning of anything in. The *Volksstem* printed a list of casualties today, and I see that our regiment lost forty-two killed at Colenso. What must the number of the wounded have been? [Here follows a list of wounded officers.] Sergeant Gage was killed, and they say he was one of the first to cross the waggon bridge. This looks as if the regiment had stormed the bridge, which is much better than being mown down in quarter column. All these losses are terrible. But I believe that Colenso is only a reconnaissance in force. What must a battle be like?

"The last week has been, if possible, more dreary than usual. One of the fellows in our room has made himself very obnoxious lately, and has had to be sat upon severely. I have never met such an ungentlemanlike creature. It is all the more unpleasant in a place like this, where we are so closely packed. There are rumours of fighting near Colesberg, probably by General French. The Boers say the action is indecisive, which means a victory for us.

"*January* 7th. — Nothing of importance has occurred lately. There has been a bit of a fight with Opperman, who tried to take away from Boshof, the local grocer, his contract for the supply of our mess, on the ground that Boshof had helped Churchill to escape: Result a complete victory for us and the reinstatement of Boshof. More Zarps, as the policemen who guard us are called, and poor little Gunning have been commandeered. He prepares himself to go. His reason is peculiar. Should his children, in after years, ask him if he fought for the freedom of the State, he would like to be able to say 'Yes'. However, if he goes I hope he will find a large rock to get behind and so come back safely.

"This afternoon a most alarming rumour was started by somebody, namely: that Ladysmith had fallen. Though I did not actually believe it, we are always having such frightful disasters that I felt very uncomfortable. Lately, however, we learned that all was well.

"*January* 10th. — Ladysmith has not fallen. The news of the defeat of the Boers on the Platrand has been confirmed, and, in spite of their lies, we know their losses were heavy. At Colesberg there was a night attack, and a half battalion of the Suffolks got much knocked about. Two of their officers came in as prisoners yesterday; they say the Boers have received large reinforcements at

Colesberg. There is a rumour that Dr. Leyds has been arrested in Germany for trying to enlist German Reservists. A British force is said to be at Douglas, west of Kimberley. They made a night attack and captured some stores and ammunition. The Transvaalers in their excitement succeeded in firing into the Free Staters, shooting, among others, Opperman's nephew. We offered our sympathies, but after all it is one the less. This evening we received a most excellent rumour that the Boers had lost 900 men near Colenso. I hope it is true, and that the Tugela has, therefore been crossed. This will be a step towards the relief of Ladysmith. At Colesberg the Boers are in a critical position. Things seem to be looking up a bit. I wish that we could get just a little truth. These rumours torture and deceive.

"*January* 29*th*. — How we clamour for news, and how our spirits rise and fall as the rumours are favourable or bad. The other day the prisoners arrived from the Spion Kop fight. The result of the attack on Spion Kop is not known. We took the hill, but, for some reason, the rumour goes that we have left it again and re-crossed the river. Can this be another lie? We heard that the regiment did not cross the waggon bridge, but tried to swim the river at Colenso last month. Very few got over. Hensley was killed the other day at Spion Kop. One can scarcely realise these losses, and I don't think we shall until we join the mess and see the sad gaps among familiar faces.

"*February* 5*th*. — We have been getting a fair share of good news lately, or, at least, good rumours. The relief of Kimberley is an established fact. Colesberg is on its last legs, though news of its surrender to French needs confirmation. There is fighting at the Tugela, concerning which the latest bulletin is 'British have taken a position — Vaal Krantz'. Nor is this all, other factors are at work besides the British Army. There is considerable dissension between the Transvaalers and the Free Staters. The former complain that they are always put in the forefront of the battle, while the latter rejoin that not only are they invariably sent to the more exposed kopjes, but that while they are aiding the Transvaalers to fight in Natal they are receiving no help in the defence of the Free State.

"*February* 12*th*. — It would take too long, even when time is nothing but a curse, to record all the items of news we have lately received. So many startling rumours have been confirmed and denied that I long to know what is the real truth, but it the Capital of this doomed country — in the very metropolis of lies and liars — we shall never learn the truth until our friends come to bring it with them.

"I have just finished reading *Esmond*, which I enjoyed very much. One advantage of my forced sojourn in this country is that I may improve my education. Indeed, reading occupies the greater part of our time though I myself cannot fix my attention on a book for very long under these miserable circumstances. The State Library has a fair selection of books, and by paying a small subscription the prisoners are allowed to take out books therefrom. The only forbidden fruits are the books of South Africa; for these volumes, recording the evil wrought by the British race on this chosen people, are carefully stowed away for fear of the English trying to destroy the histories of their crimes.

"This morning an officer of the South African Light Horse was buried. To all intents and purposes he was murdered by the Transvaal Government. Although he had typhoid fever he was thrown into prison, and not until the authorities were pretty certain he would die was he sent to the hospital. Ten officers on parole went as pall-bearers and we all subscribed for a very pretty wreath.

"Patience is played as a game here largely by ancient Colonels and Majors, and practised by us all with indifferent success as a cruel necessity.

"*February* 17*th*. — Good news at last! Kimberley has been relieved! Boers are retiring in all directions. Lord Roberts, with the British Army, has entered the Free State. Warrenton has been occupied, there is great consternation in Pretoria. Opperman is furious. Perhaps the tide has begun to turn.

"To explain how we get news: Brockie, a Sergeant-Major in the Imperial Light Horse, knows a Zarp here and gets a certain amount of news from him, which is not, however, very trustworthy. When we first came here an Englishman named Patterson, employed in the Government telegraph office, used to pass by the railings and whisper the news. He only used to come when there was good news to tell, and generally ended with the words, Hurrah, hurrah! Since he was always accompanied on these occasions by a large St. Bernard, we called him the Dogman. Lately he has elaborated and improved his system by giving us news and had begun to signal with a flag from the passage of Mr. Cullingworth's house opposite. Either he or one of the Misses Cullingworth stands some way back in the passage so as not to be visible to the Zarps and sends messages, which are read by Captain Burrows from the gymnasium window. As he is in the telegraph office and sees all that passes, the Dogman sends very truthful information

"*February* 18*th*. — More good news this morning. Cronje is lost, strayed or stolen. The Boers have been driven back at Dordrecht. The British Army is within forty miles of Bloemfontein. Buller has taken the Tugela position. All this needs no comment. '*Quo plus —*

eo plus — '. I meant to quote a Latin phrase — the only one I ever knew — but I cannot risk the tenses and moods of the verbs. It means, however, the more we have the more we want. We live, as it were, from news to news. Two officers arrived from Colesberg this morning. They say Colesberg has never been quite surrounded, only hemmed in on three sides. General French began to withdraw his cavalry about three weeks ago, sending away detachments every night until only an infantry brigade was left to sit in front of Colesberg, occupying exactly the same extent of front as before. The Boers never spotted this, so that French and his cavalry succeeded in joining the Free State column, and the infantry brigade, by making a great show of their forces, was able to keep up the ruse until the other day, when it was decided to retire. Everything went well with the retirement except for two companies of the Wiltshires who were cut off and captured after a gallant fight. I suppose all Governments lie to a certain extent about their defeats, but this Boer one takes the cake.

"*February* 19*th*. — I have caught the patience disease. I spent most of the day at this interesting game, but found by 7 p.m. I was rather sick of it. Le Mesurier told me today that Haldane, Brockie, Grimshaw and he had thought of a plane of escape. The idea was to put out the electric light in the house and in the yard by cutting the wire as it entered the building in the roof above the entrance. The sudden extinguishing of the lights on a dark night would enable them to creep to the back wall and climb over unobserved by the Zarps, whose eyes would not have become accustomed to the sudden darkness. They had made small ladders, but means of which they could climb over the corrugated iron more easily and with less noise. Once outside, they were going to trek for Mafeking, which is only about one hundred and eighty miles off. They meant to go tonight, but, though it was wet, there was too much lightning.

"*February* 21*st*. — More good news both from Stormberg and the Tugela. Our friend Opperman is getting excessively polite. I think one can best describe him as a greasy, unwashed bully, oily physically and morally, cruel to anyone in his power, cringing to those he fears.

"*February* 22*nd*. — We hear that Cronje is completely surrounded. De Wet tried to break the encircling cordon, but was defeated with great loss. Buller has taken the Boschkop and all the British troops have crossed the Tugela.

"A very amusing article appeared in one of the papers the other day, in which Napoleon was termed 'the Botha of the early '10's.' Botha the Napoleon of these days is presumption, but Napoleon, the Botha of the early '10's! I cannot help by pitying the editor of the *Volksstem*, as he is only allowed to publish good news, and must really be at his wit's-end to know what to put in now.

"Haldane and the others had arranged to go tonight, but unfortunately the sentry was walking about the place which had been chosen for getting over, so that the escape was prevented.

"*February 24th*. — Haldane and Co. have tried again. This time they were determined to go. Clough, the servant, was sent up *via* the gymnasium on to the roof to cut the wire. I gave the signal by going into the room under the main switch and asking for a map. The light went down temporarily but came up again almost immediately. We were much alarmed lest Clough should have got a shock, but he came down all right, surprised that the lights had not gone out. Of course the escape was off.

"*February 25th*. — We were all sure that Clough had not cut the wires last night. He had received a slight shock and then left it, so it was arranged that Cullen should try. However, the position of the sentry again prevented any attempt.

"*February 26th*. — Best, of the Inniskilling Fusiliers, arrived today from the Tugela. He said that all were well down there, though the fighting had been very severe, and that the troops were beyond Pieters. Cronje had no food and must surrender shortly.

"This evening the lights went out without any mistake. Opperman was greatly alarmed, and the electrician could not find out what was up. They all believed a football must have hit the wire outside and put the light out. Probably Clough had partially severed the wires, and the football had completed the damage. Now, however, the wire being broken before it was quite dark, the advantage of surprise would be lost. It was, moreover, a bright night, and we noticed that the light in the streets shone on the wall where we had meant to climb over it. The sentries were doubled, so we finally gave up the plan and tried to think of another. We are told that they will remove us to a new place on the 1st of March, and, perhaps, this will give us a better chance.

*   *   *

"When I went into my room at about 9.30 I found that Le Mesurier, Haldane, and Brockie were having a discussion. As we were to move in two days to the new prison they argued 'why not go to earth now'. The authorities would think they had escaped under cover of the light going out and would, if anything, hasten the removal of the prisoners, leaving these three under the floor to depart in peace when opportunity offered.

"*February 27th*. — This morning Opperman came into our

room as usual to count the number of prisoners in bed, and on seeing three beds empty he fairly staggered with astonishment. I was looking at him with one eye and chuckled to myself at his dismay. He went and asked Brett if he knew anything about it. Brett asked innocently, 'About what?' Then I pretended to wake up and ask Opperman what the hell he meant by disturbing us at this hour. He left the room in a fury, but presently returned with Gunning and later with Du Toit, the Chief of Police, who examined everything *à la* Sherlock Holmes, and expressed, with a smile, his confidence in the recapture of the flown birds. After breakfast the whole house was cleared and searched. The rooms, the cupboards, the roof — everywhere except under the floor. Then they brought in a dark lantern, and I really thought they had discovered the fugitives at last, but Sherlock Holmes never thought of the floor; his reasoning did not carry him there. He found Haldane's saw made out of a table knife, and connecting this with the hole in the roof of the gymnasium, the wires cut, he was sure they had gone away in the darkness. The rest, such is their mutual trust of one another in this country, were quite sure somebody had been bribed. The theories of other officers in the prison are diverting. The discussions as to how the escape had got out and where they had gone were full of imagination, but quite off the mark. In the afternoon Opperman and Sherlock Holmes came in with a hat and said the prisoners had been seen going over the hills toward Mafeking and had dropped the hat in question. By nightfall they had been tracked to Koodoosberg, about thirty miles out; and, indeed, the remains of their midday meal had been found. O wise detectives! This evening the Dogman went into Cullingworth's house in a great state of excitement and lit a candle at the verandah — a sign of good news, and on Majuba day too!

"*February* 28*th*. — We received the good news which the Dogman's excitement last night portended. Cronje has surrendered. This was received through the British Consul at Delagoa Bay. Buller has also driven back the Boers, and Botha wired: 'No use; burghers here won't face British.' In the afternoon we received the following wire: 'Cronje's surrender unconditional. Boers retreating on the Biggarsberg,' and in the evening we heard that the British were entering Ladysmith.

"Three more officers replaced the three escaped in my room. We did not let them know about those underground, but I managed to send food, news, and water down as usual, also some hot cocoa at night.

"*March* 1*st*. — Ladysmith is relieved. Joubert wires: 'On Lancers coming out of Ladysmith my mounted men retired leaving waggons and stores behind.' This afternoon the Cullingworth signalled over: 'No more news, furthest telegraph station Elandslaagte.' Kruger has gone to the front to exhort his burghers with texts. He was preceded by a telegram which was sent to all laagers. It is too long and too profane for me to copy out. Nothing but texts and psalms, showing that they are bound to win 'though the enemy compass them about', as the Almighty is their own exclusive and peculiar property. The *Volksstem* says: 'There seems to be some foundation for the rumour that Cronje has surrendered, but the report that Ladysmith has been relieved is quite untrue, our burghers are still fighting bravely south of the town. Should, however, Ladysmith be relieved, the war will only enter upon a new phase. We will then have to defend our borders against the greedy grasp of an unholy race. Now will the British see what fighting with the Boers really is. Now will the war begin in earnest.'

"(Sherlock Holmes & Co. are completely off the track and all is well below.)

"*March 2nd.* — There are no signs of our moving into our new prison. This is very disconcerting as our friends cannot stay below much longer without getting ill. The Zarps' tents have been moved into the road. Opperman says because the yard was damp, but I fancy they are afraid of an attack on the Zarps. With the dumbbells in the gymnasium it might be possible to overpower them. The day was wet and dreary; I wrote letters, Mr. Hofmeyr prayed for the escaped. I have had to divulge the secret to No. 12 room, owing to one of them unfortunately seeing the trap-door open. They were very nice about it, and will do nothing to compromise the chances of success.

"*March 6th.* — Our signals this morning informed us that the President had wired to Lord Salisbury, 'Is it not time bloodshed ceased? Will send peace proposals.' These people have got some nerve. First they declare war against an Empire, and then they expect that when they have had enough they can demand a cessation of hostilities. Three are no signs of moving.

"*March 7th.* — The Ides of March, but I don't expect Kruger will be murdered in the forum of Pretoria. Those below are still all right, though their condition is not enviable.

"*March 8th.* — The following telegrams were received today by our signaller-in-chief Burrows: (1) fighting with De Wet; (2) Occupation of Bloemfontein on the 6th. I busied myself by drawing a picture of Kruger going to the front to exhort his burghers, on the wall of my room. There seems no chance of moving. Opperman says they have not even put down the floor in our new abode. Haldane wants to try to make them move. He thought that if Grimshaw vanished too it might alarm the authorities, and make them anxious to move us to a more secure place, but I feel sure — and Grimshaw agrees with me — this would only lead to the discovery of everything.

"*March 11th*. — I drew another large picture on my wall, a sequel to the first. It represents Kruger just escaping from Lord Roberts, who with drawn sword appears to be running after him at a good pace. My picture No. 1 is entitled 'President Kruger goes to front to exhort his burghers'; No. 2, 'But returns on urgent business'.

"As chances of a move seem so uncertain and they are all determined below not to give in, it has been decided to try to get out by making a shallow tunnel, roofed in with cupboard shelves, into the hospital. Haldane is making arrangements with No. 12 room, who, it appears, are following the same plan.

"*March 12th*. — The man who came for grocery orders reported this morning that Bloemfontein has fallen, but our signal was that the British were within seven miles of the Free State capital. Opperman saw my portraits of Kruger this morning; I am afraid he did not appreciate them as he should have done. However, I told him that with a pail of whitewash and a brush he might obliterate them if he chose. (N.B. — Such is the procrastinating nature of these Boer-Hollander people that Opperman never had the pictures removed, and this with other things had, I believe, a good deal to do with his own eventual removal.)

"No. 12 decided to have nothing more to do with the digging plan. We have therefore arranged that Grimshaw, Garvice, and I shall take part in the operation. Garvice has not been informed of Le Mesurier's whereabouts, but has decided to dig. The Colonials in No. 12 room are also digging, but theirs is to be a deep tunnel and I doubt if they can master the water question.

"*March 13th*. — Tragedy. The Dogman and Cullingworth have been commandeered as undesirables, but intend, I fancy, to escape to the British lines. We signalled to him. 'Good-bye, eternal gratitude; God bless you!' The Dogman replied, 'British twenty miles north of Bloemfontein; Goodbye; speedy release; will return with Bobs.'

"We started our shaft under the big room No. 16. Apparently we made a good deal of noise, for the old Colonels were very much alarmed and threatened to stop all digging, though they did not know who the culprits were. Opperman came into the room when mining was in full swing below, and it was all the occupants could do to hustle him outside, drowning the noise of the pick by stamping. We were rather distressed and decided to wait a few days. Garvice was very much startled when he saw Le Mesurier. He describes his feelings vividly. On going down by the trap-door he remarked what an awful hole it was. Suddenly, in the flickering candle-light he saw a gaunt, bearded, unwashed face, and a half-naked body. At first he could not make out what it was, but when he at last realised it was a brother officer he said you could have knocked him down with a feather had it not been that he was already crawling on his stomach. The new shaft is a long way off; when I went down I had to crawl on hands and knees along passages and through man-holes, backwards and forwards in a regular maze of compartments, and, indeed, had the candle gone our one could easily have been lost. Haldane looked very ill, but the others, except for being covered with dirt, seemed well enough.

"*March* 14*th*. — Grimshaw went down this evening to hold a confab. They have managed to dig without making a noise by wetting the earth. Grimshaw and I made the trap-door into one piece by securing the planks together, and also made it so as to batten down from underneath. I sent them down jugs of water during the day to wash in.

"*March* 15*th*. — All went as usual this morning. Grimshaw descended and did a little digging. In the afternoon Opperman brought the news that we were to be moved tomorrow! Most of the officers were very annoyed, but Grimshaw and I sent the information below with gladness. Well, there was no time to be lost. Food enough to last them a week, all the bottles filled with water, and everything that could possibly be of any use to the cave-men was sent down. We heard, however, and not to our surprise, that others were thinking of going into their respective holes so as to escape after we had moved. As this could have had no other effect than to cause the discovery of all, we were determined if possible to stop it. We told Colonel Hunt, and he managed to persuade all concerned to abandon their schemes.

"This settled, we set to work, after final goodbyes and hand-shakings, to putty up the cracks between the boards of the trap-door, which had already been fastened down from underneath. This we succeeded in doing to perfection, and after covering the place well with dust, the trap-door could scarcely have been located by anyone; certainly not by those who did not know of its existence.

*   *   *

"*March 16th*. — The State Model School at an early hour was more than usually busy. We were all packing up such belongings as we had. I rolled everything in my mattress and rugs, and secured with rope. Then the gates were opened and all baggage was moved out on the road ready to be packed on the trolleys provided for the occasion. To be outside those gates was to breathe fresh air; to pass those barriers which had so long defied our efforts and out wits was like going our into another world. I went back into my room, and by pre-arranged taps on the floor Grimshaw signalled that all was well. I then sang 'For Auld Lang Syne' as a parting farewell.

"The Government had generously provided cabs for the convenience of the officers (who afterwards found they had to pay), and at about 10 a.m. the first cabs rolled off amid the friendly farewells of many neighbours. The long column of vehicles was escorted by a motley guard, consisting of very old men and tiny boys armed with Sniders and sporting guns of ancient pattern.

"We soon passed out of the town and, crossing a small river, began to crawl up a steep hill. The roads outside of Pretoria appear very much neglected, but, of course, the money that should have been devoted to general improvements was all spent in secret service or in preparations for the war. We soon arrived at our destination. The building stands halfway up the side of a hill, and is probably a much healthier place than the Model School. Besides, the view is really pretty. To the north, indeed, it is limited by the tops of two hills. Southward lies Pretoria, a collection of large Government buildings and of small villas amid masses of trees, nestling beneath a high range of hills, along the crest of which rise the famous forts. The view on the west is merely a vast plain which reaches to the horizon, and a large hill obliterates any view to the east.

"The place itself consists merely of a long white shanty with a fairly large compound enclosed by formidable barbed-wire entanglements. Outside are Opperman's house and the Zarps' tents. There are electric lights all round the enclosure, making escape a matter of considerable difficulty. Inside, the place looked more like a cattle-shed than anything else. A long galvanised-iron building, divided into sleeping-room, and four small bath-rooms, a servants' compartment and kitchen, eating-rooms. The sleeping-hall is eighty-five by thirty yards long and accommodates 120 officers, our beds being, roughly, a yard apart. There is no flooring. The drains consist of open ditches, while the sanitary arrangements are enough to disgust any civilised being. A strong protest was at once sent in to the authorities, but I doubt that it will have any effect.

"*March* 18*th*. — The greatest disadvantage of this place over the State Model School is that we can get no news.

"*March* 22*nd*. — Gunning gave us a small baboon the other day, which was very fierce at first, but has tamed wonderfully. There are many different kinds of curious insects here — not curious for this country, of course, but which I have never seen before. The 'Praying Mantis' or 'Kaffir God' is one of the queerest. The whole place seems to be a large ants' nest, and we have often witnessed great fights between the different kinds. Snakes also abound. A night-adder was killed the other day. It was about thirteen or fourteen inches long and very poisonous, so Gunning says.

"We hear Gunning and Opperman are going to the front to-morrow. I am very sorry for the former, though the departure of the latter is a great advantage.

"*March* 23*rd*. — The Zarps and Opperman departed for the front this morning. Their place was taken by a new guard selected from the Hollander Corp. The Commandant is a pleasant fellow and a great improvement on Opperman.

"*March* 25*th*. — We had service as usual this morning. This evening an attempt to escape was going to be made by Ansell and Co., but it never came off. There has been no news of Haldane and the others, so I suppose they are well away by now. This evening the new Commandant had roll-call. We call him 'Pyjamas', because he wears a suit of clothes for all the world like a pair of pyjamas. His real name is Westernant.

"*March* 30*th*. — There has not been anything very important to record for some days. On Tuesday an attempt to escape was made by Best. While one sentry was gossiping with another he crept under the barbed wire. As luck would have it, when Best had got half way through, the sentry finished his *tête-à-tête* and returned to his post. At first he thought Best was a dog and called out *footsack* (be off), but seeing he was a human being, merely told him to go back. He might have shot him with some excuse, so Best was lucky in striking a kind-hearted man.

"On Wednesday Joubert died. In respect to him we sent a wreath. I don't think this will have any effect on the war, as (and the papers say as much) his moderate attitude in the recent crisis had taken away much of his popularity.

"*April* 3*rd*. — Hurrah! the papers this evening report the safe arrival of Haldane, Le Mesurier and Brockie at Lourenço Marques, having travelled through Swaziland. We were so glad to hear this news. Alas! We also hear that sixteen officers arrive tomorrow, and that seven guns were captured with them.

"The Cullingworth girls came up this evening and signalled with a handkerchief that Mafeking had been relieved. I hope it is true. We all admire the pluck of those girls. We have already collected a large subscription to get them and the Dogman handsome presents.

"There was a large swarm of locust yesterday. So thick was the cloud that it quite obliterated the view of the distant hills. They continued passing over nearly all day.

"*April 5th.* — The prisoners arrived this morning. They mostly belong to 'U' Battery, R.H.A.; some to the M.I. and cavalry. I have not quite gathered the circumstances of their capture, but they seem to have been caught in a trap, owing to the want of the ordinary precautions. The convoy and one battery were practically held up without firing a shot, but the other battery got away. When marched off they heard that another British force was pursuing so that the guns may be recaptured.

"They bring very little news; apparently they have heard nothing about the relief of Mafeking, though Warren was on his way thereto. Roberts has been delayed in his advance for the want of horses, but as this has been remedied the forward movement should begin shortly. Had the horses not been so done after Abram's Kraal, they say De Wet would have been caught and the war over. Such is the fashion of war. If so-and-so had happened — always 'if'!

"There was great excitement this evening caused by an attempted escape. The electric wire had been tampered with, and at about 10.30, by some device, Horne, a colonial, who is also an electrician, made the current travel on a shorter circuit, thus blowing out the main fuse and extinguishing all the lights round the building. Hardly had this happened than two shots were fired in quick succession, and then another. The escape failed, but all got back into the building unwounded. Apparently the light had gone down, then up for a second, then finally out.

"During the momentary flash Hockley, of the escapees, had been seen and fired at. However, 'All's well that ends well', though some say that two bullets went through the dining-room. Sentries were doubled for the night and patrols sent out.

"*April 6th.* — How the fortunes of war vary! We seem to be going through a series of small disasters. Today the papers have the report of a 'Brilliant Boer Victory, thirty-six miles south-east of Bloemfontein; 450 prisoners!!!' The only hope is that the account is not 'official'. But we must be ready for the worst. The leading article says: 'Within a few days Roberts will be forced to evacuate the Free

State. *His retreat from Bloemfontein will be like Napoleon's retreat from Moscow.'*

"*April 11th.* — The prisoners reported captured some time ago have not arrived yet. They always seem to be 'expected to arrive somewhere', but apparently have not yet been actually seen by anybody. On Saturday their capture was reported officially. On Thursday English wires said that 300 Royal Irish were surrounded. Today they say the prisoners are expected at Pretoria tomorrow! Well, we shall see.

"The last few days we have had many good rumors about the capture of Boers and British victories. Today the papers say that Lord Methuen is advancing on Boshof (he must be there by now), and that Colonel de Villebois has been killed. He, apparently, and his men (100, so they say — probably 500) were all killed, wounded, or taken prisoners. A distinguished ex-French officer and his foreign legion is a good bag.

"The next piece of information is, quoting from Boer paragraphs or headlines, 'Fifteen hundred English in a corner'; 'Brabant's Horse in a trap'. Then, again, 'There is every hope of their surrender'. So much for this. But on the Dutch side we read that all telegraphic communication with Ladybrand and the south has been cut, so I rather fancy the Boers have over-reached themselves for once.

"The Boers have attacked our camps at Elandslaagte, and because, when they shelled, our camp tents were struck, they report that the British fled. I wonder if Le Mesurier was in this show.

"In all these fights, as usual, the Boers 'By the grace of God had (about) one man killed and four wounded,' This is heavy; generally it is one horse and three mules. 'The enemy', of course, 'must have lost heavily.' So the paragraphs run on. Many are the funny expressions. 'One brave burgher succumbed to the explosion of a bomb.' 'One of our guns *in firing* damaged its sight and one of its wheels!' They always end up with 'Our burghers are full of courage, and determined to withstand the enemy to the last.'

"Various officials came up the day before yesterday to inquire into the causes of the protest we had sent in, signed by all the officers here. They promised that everything would be seen to; but they are all — well they are Boer officials, and I doubt if our lot is to be in any way improved.

"The weather is getting much colder now, though the sun is still hot by day. A few stray shots whistled over the building today, probably 'accidentally on purpose'. I hope they do not begin sniping regularly.

"*April 12th*. — Alas! my hopes were doomed to disappointment. Eight prisoners arrived. They are mostly of the Irish Rifles; unlucky regiment, twice the victims of misfortune! There is among them a gunner who was acting on the staff. As usual, they bring little news, except a vivid account of their own 'show', which happened when they were on a bill-posting expedition.[3] A cart-load of packing cases came in today for the prisoners of war. Seven tons have already been sent to Waterval. These cases contained papers, books, cigars, cigarettes, tobacco and groceries, of which we were very thankful, the more so to feel the people at home had not forgotten the unhappy prisoners of war.

"Since the new year one of the chief topics of discussion and bets has been: 'When the war will be over.' We have, alas! always underestimated the length of our say here; had the prophecies of the more sanguine come true, we would have been free long ago. Some put the date of our release at the Queen's birthday; others later, and a few earlier. Personally, I have learnt since I have been here the impossibility of predicting what the future has in store. The day will surely come, though would that we knew the date, be it months hence, for we might then cross off the days as they passed.

"*April 17th*. — The papers have given no news for a considerable time. But rumours of the wildest description have been spread. Ever since Friday last rumour has persisted in De Wet's capture, and, indeed, it seems possible, even probable; having succeeded in two captures, General De Wet was not likely to be allowed to take another bag without some counter move on Lord Roberts's part. The papers today say nothing on the English side about De Wet, except that no news has been got, or, indeed, can be got, from the lost General. Rumour also has it that Lukas Meyer has been captured on the Natal side.

"I have been continuing my sketched and caricatures pretty regularly. I have also been reading more lately. Being Easter week, Mr. Hofmeyr held a service on Good Friday, and administered the Holy Communion on Easter Sunday. Easter Sunday! If somebody had told me when first captured that I should still be in prison on Easter Sunday, I should have thought him mad, or expected to go mad myself. 'Tis well we know not the future, but always live on hopes of early release.

"I have written and received a good many letters. I think I am

3   Distributing the proclamation.

quite reforming in the way of letter writing — that is, I am getting into the way of writing four pages of tolerably sensible stuff on nothing at all, which is a sure sign of a good correspondent.

"Talking of being a prisoner, we have heard more of those fortunate escaped. Fortunate! One cannot but think them lucky, and envy them, now they are free, with the just credit for their escape. But how many hardships had they to suffer? Well, to come to the point. Davy has just returned from hospital, where he saw Haldane's account of his escape in the *Standard and Diggers' News*. The trains did not seem to fit in, and our friends had a lot of walking to do. Le Mesurier sprained his ankle; food ran out, and they had to live on Kaffir food. Finally, getting into a coal truck, where they were nearly discovered, they crossed the border at Komati Poort. I envy them; but such success cannot be got without daring. Luck has certainly followed them, but I think their patience underground won Fortune's favour.

"We hear from Davy that the Dogman and Cullingworth are prisoners, having been arrested when trying to escape to the British lines. Poor fellows! Though, as our friends at home say of us, 'They are safer in prison than at the front.' This saying always irritates me. Every letter hints at it, as if safety were the chief reward one hoped to get during a war; one cannot help feeling bitter, though our imprisonment is only a payment for our very lives.

"*April* 19*th*. — Roulette is in full swing here. The arrangements are most ingenious and the dining-room after dinner is a regular Monte Carlo.

"We had a large mess meeting today to appoint a new mess committee, and to discuss various questions as regards the expenses, &c. It was a very amusing assembly, rather too frivolous to carry any real motions. Most of the speeches wandered off the point, and we finally dispersed without deciding anything of importance. One thing was, however, serious. Colonel Hunt appealed for further subscriptions for the sick soldiers in hospital. They are apparently supported by charity, and by our subscriptions. The Transvaal Government (although boasting to be civilised) does not even supply beds! This fact might, perhaps, disillusion some who are so taken in by Boer cant.

"*May* 8*th*. — We have had an immense amount of news lately. Roberts has begun his big advance. Brandfort is in our hands also Winburg. The force advancing *via* Boshof has reached Hoopstad, while the British have crossed the Vaal at Fourteen Streams. De Wet has not been heard of for a considerable time. So much is acknowledged in the papers. Rumours say that we are behind Kroonstadt!!

That De Wet, Steyn, and 8,000 Boers have been taken!! The English in the town think we shall be released by the 24th of May. A panic seems to have seized the Boers, and excited meetings have been held. Kruger summoned the Volksraad on Sunday, and addressed them in stirring words, which, while acknowledging the serious nature of the situation, exhorted the burghers to continue the struggle trusting in the Lord. General Schalk Burger, while addressing the townspeople, said that a stand might yet be made, if not, the independence of the Republic was at an end. The Church of Pretoria has addressed petitions for peace to the Churches of Great Britain and of Europe and America. They pray that this unholy bloodshed may cease. Kruger says 'Continue the struggle to the end.' Is it for England or for Kruger to give in?

"We have started a newspaper; it is progressing. We call it the *Gram*, because at the State Model School all our news comes in under the popular names of signal-gram (when news was signalled), Kaffir-gram (when brought through the Kaffir). Brockie-gram (when Brockie succeeded in getting information from the Zarps), and so forth. Rosslyn is editor; Major Sturges sub-editor. White, R.A., Wake, 5th Fusiliers, and I, are the artists. The paper has been all written out by Rosslyn, and is now being hektographed. We hope to bring out seventy good copies of the first number.

"*May 13th*. — Though two or three prisoners have arrived lately, we can get no particular details of the news. There is no doubt that a general advance has been begun, but what point our troops have reached is uncertain. Also, it is still a question whether De Wet is captured or not. This morning the most serious rumour came in, to the effect that Mafeking had fallen, but I can scarcely believe it.

"Yesterday Mr. Hofmeyr received the welcome order to pack up his things and go. He seemed very affected at saying goodbye and nearly broke down. We all liked him very much, and bade him a hearty farewell, cheering him as he left the enclosure, and singing 'He's a jolly good fellow.' We shall miss him as well as his services.

"Our paper came out yesterday and was a great success. We hope to bring out a new one on the Queen's Birthday, though it is an awful labour.

"Life has not been so bad lately. Buoyed up with hope of a speedy release, and occupied with the *Gram*, time has passed, in my case, more quickly. We had a selling lottery the other day for the day of our release. The dates ranged from the 15th of May to the 15th of August. The Queen's Birthday was much in request, while 'the field' (any day after August 15ht) went for six pounds.

"The *Volksstem*, of course, progressed as usual. Having exhausted all other insults on England, they commenced lately on the Queen! During the present British advance the mendacious powers of the editor are once more brought to trial, and once more he has not been found wanting. The burghers are full of courage (running everywhere); even the women wish to fight! There was, indeed, a rumour that our present guard was to be commandeered and the women put here to look after us. Poor time for us! I fancy we should be all shot! The Volksraad sat the other day, and after Kruger and others quoting a few scriptures the session of 1900 was closed after sitting two days!

"*May* 14th. — So much news has arrived today that I think I had better inscribe it, while I remember. This morning came the rumour that a good many Boers actually did get into Mafeking, but, being unsupported, still remain there. This evening's *Volksstem* is truly a wonder. It gives more news than it ever has given before. An attack was made on Mafeking. The Boers took a 'fort', but were attacked by night, and lost seven killed and 'some' wounded and prisoners. At present Carrington and Plumer are proceeding to Mafeking by train, so that it must have been relieved. Everywhere the Boers fly, and the British troops entered Kroonstadt on the 11th inst. Hunter, with his 25,000 men, drove the enemy back at Warrenton, and 'the Boers are unable to resist the advance of the forces at Vryberg'.

"'But,' says the *Volksstem*, 'the fact that Kroonstadt is in the hands of the enemy need create no alarm. As we retire our line of defence becomes less and our commandos can be concentrated to resist more effectually the advance of the British forces. Besides, many things may happen which will put an entirely new face on the war. Our delegation has reached America, &c., &c. Lord Roberts's hastened advance is said to be caused by his desire to reach Pretoria on the Queen's Birthday, but might not the real reason be the fear of foreign intervention? Lord Roberts wishes to strike a decisive blow before his forces are needed elsewhere. Every day's delay is, therefore, an advantage to our cause. Courage is all that is needed, &c. &c.;

"The above is a précis of the *Volksstem* leading article. Still they harp on foreign intervention, but from what I gather from recent Continental criticisms on the war, I fancy their chances in this line are less than at the beginning of the war. As to the burghers' courage, I doubt if the majority of them have much left. For many months the Transvaal Government have whipped their subjects to the fight; but even the worm will turn, and to the simplest, or the most ignorant, the Government promises and hopes must seem vain.

"The day of our release is, perhaps, approaching; but it does not do to be too sanguine; one never knows where a check may occur. Still I 'plump' on the end of the present month.

"*May 20th*. — The month is drawing to a close, and the day of our release is still a matter of speculation. News is pretty plentiful; even the *Volksstem* tries to hide nothing. Roberts has made a great advance, but whether he has halted at Kroonstadt or not is uncertain. We all hoped he would not stop until he had reached Pretoria.

"We have been very much alarmed lately at the rumoured intention of the Government to move us to Lydenburg, but at present it is only a rumour. If we are moved we shall have every prospect of being shunted about the country with guerilla bands of Boers who would keep us merely as hostages. If, however, we are kept here we shall have every chance of being released during siege of Johannesburg. The Boers, it is said, have decided to hold that place and are not going to blow up the mines. The defence of Pretoria would be impossible with the troops at their disposal.

"Life goes on as usual. The only diversion that has lately occurred was the athletic sport, which were got up by some energetic people. The event took place yesterday, and, on the whole, was a decided success. The chief feature, however, of the day was the betting. Several enterprising officers kept books, but Haig, of the Inniskilling Dragoons, cut the best figure in that line, and it was chiefly owing to his amusing performance that the day was a success. White has made an excellent sketch of 'Our Bookie' for the next *Gram* number.

"The sermon this morning is worth recording. The Rev. Mr. Bateman delivered a most extraordinary speech as part of his service. Whether it was meant for our spiritual edification, or merely intended to convey news to us under the disguise of a text, was not quite certain; but, by preaching on the text that begins 'As cold water is to the thirsty soul, so is good news, &c.', he led us to believe that we were to be released in a very short time.

"Roulette has been going very strong. Large sums have been lost and won."

"*May 25th*. — Yesterday we prisoners of war joined with the British Empire all over the world in the celebration of the Queen's Birthday. In our little enclosure we have quite a representative British Empire — English, Scotch, and Irish soldiers, Colonials, South Africans, Australians, and civilians, and, indeed, we only require a Canadian to complete the list.

"Yesterday evening we drank the Queen's health in light port (rather nasty). The first drops of wine or spirit I had tasted since the 18th of November, This was followed by 'God Save the Queen,' sung by all with a heartiness and feeling that I never heard before. It must have sounded very well outside. To us it was as it were 'giving vent' to our imprisoned feelings, while we also found in it a link with our country, from which we have so many months been severed.

"It is now pretty certain that Roberts is resting his troops, and rumours have it that the Boers have asked for an armistice. Whether Lord Roberts celebrated the Queen's Birthday by a victory or a peaceful armistice remains to be seen.

"The *Volksstem* considered that it would be a graceful act on the part of the State President if he were to wire the Queen and offer her as a birthday present the unconditional release of all the British prisoners of war. As the *Volksstem* is the official organ, this may quite possible be merely a feeler to the public (if public there be in this country). At any rate it would be an act worthy of the wily Boer. He finds it a source of trouble and expense feeding and guarding 5,000 prisoners, so he gives them away with a pound of tea — I mean as a graceful act. Whether the offer would be accepted is uncertain. But we at any rate will be very happy if the Transvaal Government puts us over the border.

"The weather (by day) is simply perfect. Every morning the lovely air makes one long for a walk or ride, and causes one to chafe at the inability to roam beyond the one hundred yards' enclosure. We are henceforth to be allowed to have wine, but personally I shall wait for freedom before I indulge in that luxury again. The second number of the *Gram* came out yesterday, and, I believe, was much appreciated.

"*May 26th.* — Two prisoners of war arrived this morning. They were caught at Lindley, which the Boers have apparently reoccupied. They were taken across country to the Natal railway, and then conveyed straight to Pretoria. They say they have heard firing at the Vaal, so I suppose Lord Roberts is there. The Boers hold a strong position south of Johannesburg, and they also intend defending that town. One of the De Wets is still on the right rear of our army, but will be dealt with by Rundle's division which is coming up that way. It is said that De Wet at one time offered to surrender on condition that he himself should not be made a prisoner. But Roberts would receive none but an unconditional surrender. Buller has been ordered to force Laing's Nek at all costs. The *Volksstem* says that Lord Roberts's headquarters are at Honningspruit, some way north of Kroonstadt, but this is probably news of some days' standing. There is also a rumour that our troops have occupied Potchef-stroom.

"*May 29th*. — At last our release seems near at hand. Yesterday and today big guns were heard plainly in the direction of Johannes-burg, which is now in our hands. Boshof, the grocer, has just arrived, having come up by the last train. He says that the Dragoons were actually in the streets when he left. I fancy tomorrow or next day will see us out. Everybody is in the best of spirits and full of excitement.

"Greatest excitement during dinner. Mr. Hay and Mr. Wood came in and asked Colonel Hunt to send twenty-four officers to Waterval to look after the men. Kruger has gone to Holland. The British are expected here tomorrow, and we shall be free! We sang 'God Save the Queen' and cheered Hay and the Commandant, who made a very nice speech, saying he hoped to shake hands with us outside. Oh! How I longed to see the old regiment once more! The Commandant says that there is still fighting at Klipdrift, but I believe there is a lot of looting going on in the town now. Roulette is at an end. I can scarcely write coherently, so excited am I. Fancy being free; I can scarcely believe it! Six and a half months' imprison-ment, and about to be freed! Thank God!

"*May 31st*. — Too premature were our hopes. Yesterday and today have been spent in awful suspense. Distant guns have been heard, Boers have been seen riding about, and rumours of all kinds and descriptions are rife. It is too awful this final suspense. We do nothing in hope of a speedy release, and we pass the day anxiously scanning the horizon for the approach of troops.

"All day commandos in from Mafeking. One commando came up our way, and we were rather surprised that they made no attempt to shoot us. Indeed there was nothing to prevent them. Three pris-oners came in. They were caught in or near Johannesburg. That town was officially surrendered at 10 a.m. this morning. The Boers intend making a sort of stand (one of their usual ten-minute affairs I suppose) at Irene, a place six miles south of Pretoria, and a fight is expected there tomorrow. Their line of flight is past our abode and Waterval, and I should not be surprised if, unable to face and shoot armed men, some of these foreign ruffians shoot a few prisoners.

"The town is evidently to be handed over quietly. The *Volksstem* is still covering a sheet of paper with print, but seems to take not the slightest interest in the war. They speak of giving up Pretoria as one of our papers might of a concert. Well, I suppose it will come at last, but I shall heave a sigh of relief when it does!

"*June 1st*. — No sign of the British! But we expect to hear guns tomorrow. There are plenty of rumours about — Roberts captured, French killed, &c. There was a good deal of looting in the town yesterday, and five men were shot. Our hopes of a few days ago have been somewhat damped, and most of us put our release down at a week hence.

"The *Volksstem* is remarkable. The editor is evidently wishful to avoid his tarring and feathering, and scarcely speaks of the war at all.

"*June 3rd.* — I have almost given up looking forward to our release, and have fallen back into the ordinary monotonous life. No guns have been heard, and therefore no serious fighting can have taken place anywhere near Pretoria. Rundle has been reported as having received a check in the Free State, and Lord Roberts is said to be still in Johannesburg; otherwise there is no news at all. Botha has taken matters into his own hands, has kicked out the officials appointed by Kruger, chosen a committee of his own, and has arranged the defence of the positions outside the town. He has therefore made himself practically President of what remains of the Transvaal. Kruger went off with a million of hard gold, paying the Government officials with dishonoured cheques on the National Bank, from which he has removed all the money. Every one of his ministers thirsts for the old man's blood, and perhaps it were best for him to go further than Middelburg.

"*June 4th.* — At about 8.30 this morning firing was heard at no great distance, in the south-west direction — field guns, 'pom-poms', Maxims, and even musketry. At about nine o'clock a shell was seen to burst on an earthwork on a ridge of hill south of the town. Field-glasses and telescopes were immediately brought out, and we were well entertained for the rest of the day. Shrapnel burst all along the ridges, and presently lyddite shells were planted on the hills. The firing seemed very unmethodical, and the Boers made little or no reply. On the western kopjes shrapnel was seen bursting all over the place, and we expected the Infantry to attack them. But the lyddite shells were certainly most interesting. They burst with a tremendous noise, throwing up clouds of brownish earth. For some time the forts seemed to be the mark our gunners were aiming at, and these costly erections certainly received their share — four shells pitching well inside the west fort; but, later, the shells were directed on the eastern outskirts of the town. Whether these were intended for the railway station, we could not make out; but, otherwise, they seemed to have no object. At about 4.30 the Boers were seen leaving the western ridges and trekking at a remarkable pace across the plain, disappearing along the northern road. The day's action was ended by a kind of *feu de joie* of lyddite shells, which struck the two forts and the surrounding hills. Then peace ensued. The last few shots seemed to have been fired by guns which were much closer than at the commencement of the bombardment, and the flight of the projectiles, which we could distinctly hear, passed from west to east, so that we hoped our troops have occupied the hills on the west.

"The hills are burning tonight, and the scene is strangely illuminated in honour of our approaching rescue.

"*June 5th*. — A day of strangely mingled hopes and fears. This morning at about 1.30 the Commandant awoke us and ordered us to pack up at once and prepare to march to the railway, whence we were to be transported by train down the Delagoa Bay line to some station beyond Middelburg. All were filled with consternation. To be hurried away when release was so near at hand seemed too awful. Words cannot express my feelings. At last we decided to refuse to go. Let them massacre us if they dared. We reminded the Commandant of the promise made to the officers the week before that if they restrained the men in Waterval neither they nor the men should be transported. The Commandant replied that he had his orders and must execute them, and he rose to leave the building, but we refused to let him or his lieutenant go, and held them both prisoners. The Commandant said that the guards would soon come in to rescue him, but he eventually promised to do his best to save us from being deported, if we set him free. Then, by Colonel Hunt's advice, for we did not know when a commando might appear, we returned to bed — you cannot shoot men in their beds. And so passed the anxious hours away till dawn. With the first streaks of daylight we scanned the hills anxiously for the British troops. We could see lines of men moving on the race-course, but it was impossible to make out what they were. Presently, at about half-past eight, two figures in khaki came round the corner, crossed the little brook and galloped towards us. Were they Boers come to order our removal? — the advance scouts, perhaps, of a commando to enforce the order! — or were they our friends at last? Yes, thank God! One of the horsemen raised his hat and cheered. There was a wild rush across the enclosure, hoarse discordant yells, and the prisoners tore like madmen to welcome the first of their deliverers.

"Who should I see on reaching the gate but Churchill, who, with his cousin, the Duke of Marlborough, had galloped on in front of the army to bring us the good tidings. It is impossible to describe our feelings on being freed. I can scarcely believe it, after seven months' imprisonment, the joy nearly made up for all our former troubles, and, besides, the war is not yet over.

"To close the scene we hoisted the Union Jack which Burrows (one of the prisoners) had made by cutting up a Vierkleur, on the staff whence the Transvaal colours had so long reminded us of our condition. I will not write about the triumphal entry of Lord Roberts and the army into Pretoria, because that has been already told by so many others.

"The Dogman and Cullingworth shared our good fortune, both being speedily released from the gaol where they had languished since their attempt to get through to the British lines, and with this happy fact let me end my record of so many weary days passed in uncertainty, disappointment, and monotony, but borne, I hope, with patience, and ending at last in joy."

CHAPTER SEVENTEEN

ACTION OF DIAMOND HILL

Pretoria: June 14, 1900

The feeble resistance which the Boers offered to our advance from Bloemfontein favoured the hope that with the fall of Pretoria they would sue for peace, and after the almost bloodless capture of the town there was a very general tendency to regard the war as practically over. The troops who had been marching for so many days with Pretoria as their goal, not unnaturally hoped that when that goal was achieved a period of rest and refreshment would be given them. But the imperious necessities of war demanded fresh efforts.

The successes gained in the Free State by the redoubtable Christiaan De Wet, and the cutting of the communications near Rhenoster, awoke everyone to the fact that further exertions were required. Though the Boers under Botha had made but a poor resistance in front of their capital, they were encouraged by the news from the Free State to adopt a more defiant attitude, and to make what we hope has been almost a final effort. As to that I will not be sanguine; but it is certain that, whereas on the 7th and 8th of June the Boer leaders in the Transvaal were contemplating surrender, on the 9th and 10th they were making all kinds of bold schemes to harass and even entrap the British army.

On the 7th the news ran through the camp that Mrs. Botha had come through the lines with some mission on her husband's behalf, and General Schoeman had himself made very decided overtures. On the 8th, therefore, an armistice was observed by both sides, and a conference on Zwartskop, where Lord Roberts was to meet the Republican generals, was arranged for the 9th; but when the 9th came circumstances had changed. The Field-Marshal had actually his foot in the stirrup ready to ride to the meeting-place, when a messenger arrived from Botha declining, unless Lord Roberts had some new proposal to make, to enter into any negotiations. The consequence of this was an immediate resumption of active operations.

The military situation was, briefly, that Lord Roberts's army was spread around and in Pretoria in various convenient camping grounds, with the greater part of its force displayed on the east and north-east sides of the town; and that the Boers, under Botha and

De la Rey, to the number of about 7,000, with twenty-five guns, held a strong position some fifteen miles to the east astride the Delagoa Bay Railway. It was evident that on any grounds, whether moral or material, it was not possible for the conquering army to allow the capital to be perpetually threatened by the enemy in organised force, and, indeed, to be in a state of semi-siege.

With the intention, therefore, of driving the enemy from the neighborhood, and in the hope of capturing guns and prisoners, a large series of combined operations was begun. Practically all the available troops were to be employed. But the army which had marched from Bloemfontein had dwindled seriously from sickness, from casualties, and, above all, from the necessity of dropping brigades and battalions behind it to maintain the communications. We have already seen how it was necessary to leave the Fourteenth Brigade to hold Johannesburg, and now the Eighteenth Brigade became perforce the garrison of Pretoria, thus leaving only the Eleventh Division, the corps troops, and Ian Hamilton's force free for field operations.

The Eleventh Division numbered, perhaps, 6,000 bayonets with twenty guns. Ian Hamilton's force had lost Smith-Dorrien's Brigade, which was disposed along the line between Kroonstadt and Pretoria, and though strengthened by the addition of Gordon's Calvary Brigade did not number more than 3,000 bayonets, 1,000 sabres, and 2,000 rifle-armed cavalry, with thirty guns. But the shrinkage had been greatest among the mounted troops. French's command of a Cavalry Division, which should have been some 6,000 mounted men, was scarcely, even with part of Hutton's Brigade of Mounted Infantry, 2,000. The two cavalry brigades with Ian Hamilton mustered together only 1,100 men, and Ridley's Mounted Infantry, whose nominal strength was at least 4,000, was scarcely as strong as regiments, regiments only a little stronger than squadrons, and the pitiful — absurd if it had not been so serious — spectacle of troops of eight and ten men was everywhere to be seen. It must, therefore, be remembered that though the imposing names of divisions and brigades might seem to indicate a great and powerful force, the army at Lord Roberts's disposal was really a very small one.

The enemy's position ran along a high line of steep and often precipitous hills, which extend north and south athwart the Delagoa Bay line about fifteen miles east from Pretoria, and stretch away indefinitely on either side. The plan of the Field-Marshal was to turn both flanks with cavalry forces, and to endeavour to cur the line behind the Boers, so that, threatened by the attack of the

Infantry in front, and their retreat compromised, they would have to fall back, probably without being able to save some, at least, of their heavy guns.

French was directed to make a wide sweep round the enemy's right flank north of the railway. Pole-Carew, with the Eighteenth Brigade and the Guards, was to advance frontally along the railway; Ian Hamilton to move parallel to him about six miles further south; and Broadwood, who, with the rest of the mounted troops, formed part of Hamilton's force, was to endeavour to turn the enemy's left. It was felt that, important as were the objects to be gained, they scarcely justified a very large sacrifice of life. But though the Field-Marshal would be content with the retreat of the enemy, both Cavalry forces were intended to press hard inward.

On the 11th, the whole army was in motion. French on the extreme left of the British front, which was extended from flank to flank about sixteen miles, soon came in contact with the Boers, occupying strong defensive positions, and he became sharply engaged. During the day he continued to persevere, but it was not until nightfall that he was able to make any progress. Pole-Carew, with the Eleventh Division, moved eastward along the railway, extended in battle formation, and engaged the enemy with his long-range guns, to which the Boers replied with corresponding pieces, including a 6-in. gun mounted on a railway truck. Though an intermittent bombardment continued throughout the day, the operations in the centre were confined to a demonstration.

Meanwhile Broadwood and Ian Hamilton, advancing on the right, found that the Boers, besides occupying the whole line of the Diamond Hill plateau, had also extended their left flank, which was composed of the Heidelberg commando and other South Transvaal burghers, far beyond the reach of any turning movement, and for this reason the operations to the British right and right centre became of a piercing rather than of an enveloping nature. Hamilton endeavoured to hold off the enemy's unduly extended left by detaching a battalion, two field guns, and Gordon's Cavalry Brigade with its horse battery, in the direction of the Tigerspoort ridges. Ridley's Brigade of Mounted Infantry struck out, like the arms of a swimmer. Broadwood's Brigade was intended to push through the gap thus made.

A dropping musketry and artillery fire began shortly after eight o'clock along the front of the force engaged in containing the Boers near Tigerspoort, and half an hour later Ridley's Brigade was engaged along the southern slopes of Diamond Hill. Meanwhile, Broadwood was advancing steadily to the eastward, and crossing a difficult spruit debouched into a wide, smooth, grass plain, surrounded by hills of varying height, at the eastern end of which was a narrow gap. Through this the line of march to the railway lay. He became immediately engaged with the Boers round the whole three-quarters of the circle; and a scattered action, presenting to a distant observer no picturesque features, and yet abounding in striking incidents, began. The Boers brought seven guns, so far as we could observe, against him, and since the fire of these pieces was of a converging nature, the cavalry was soon exposed to a heavy bombardment.

In spite of this, Broadwood continued to push on. The country was well suited for cavalry action, and the gap of "poort", as it is called in this country, plainly visible among the hills to the eastward, encouraged him to try to break through. Accordingly, at about eleven o'clock, he brought two horse-guns, under Lieutenant Con-

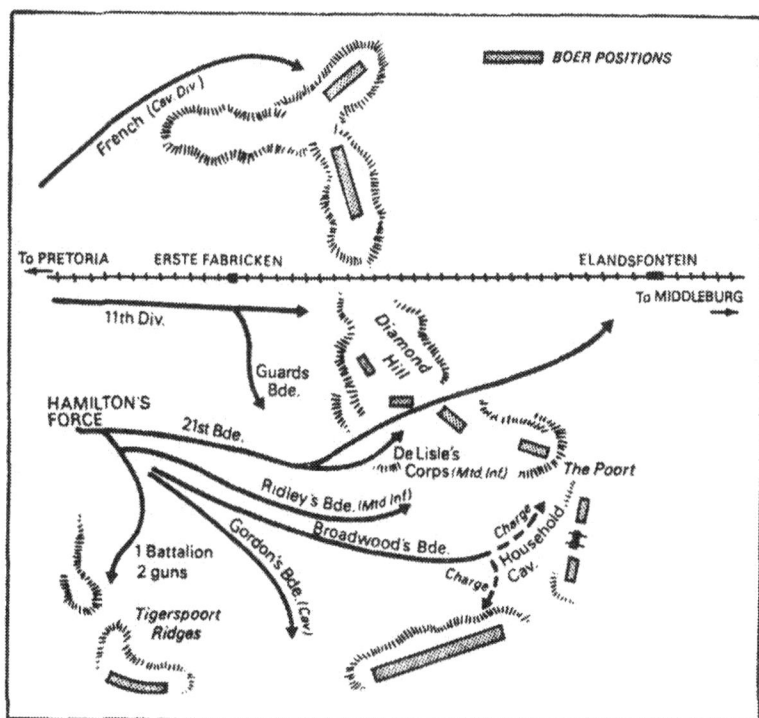

PLAN OF THE OPERATIONS OF 11TH AND 12TH JUNE, 1900

nolly,[4] into a very forward position, with the design of clearing his road by their fire. The Boers, however, fought with a stubbornness and dash which had long been absent from their tactics. They were in this part of the field largely composed of Germans and other foreigners, of colonial rebels, and of various types of irreconcilables.

No sooner had these two guns come into action that a very ugly attack was made on them. The ridge from which they were fighting was one of those gentle swells of ground which, curving everywhere, nowhere allows a very extended view; and the Boers, about 200 strong, dashed forward with the greatest boldness in the hope of bringing a close musketry fire to bear on the gunners and of capturing their pieces. So sudden was the attack that their heads were seen appearing over the grass scarcely 300 yards away. In these circumstances the guns fired case shot, but though they prevented the Boers from coming nearer, it was evident that the position was still critical. Broadwood was compelled, therefore, to ask the 12th Lancers to charge.

The continual shrapnel fire of the last few hours had, in spite of their dispersed formation, caused a good deal of loss among the horses of the brigade. The Earl of Airlie, who was riding with the brigadier, had had his horse shot under him, and had gone away to find another. He returned to place himself at the head of his regiment just as it was moving forward to the attack, and, perhaps unacquainted with the latest development of the action, he gave a direction to the charge which was slightly more northerly than that which Broadwood intended; so that, in advancing, the regiment gradually came under the fire of the enemy holding the lower slopes of Diamond Hill, instead of falling on those who were directly threatening the guns. But it was a fine, gallant manœuver, executed with a spring and an elasticity wonderful and admirable in any troops, still more in troops who have been engaged for eight months in continual fighting with an elusive enemy, and who must have regarded any action, subsequent to the capture of Pretoria, rather in the nature of an anti-climax.

Its effect was instantaneous. Though the regiment scarcely numbered 150 men, the Boers fled before them — those who were threatening the guns towards the south, and those immediately in

---

4   A younger brother of that brilliant officer of the Scots Greys, whose death at Nitral Nek a few weeks later was so great a loss to his friends, his regiment, and his country.

the line of the charge eastward and northward, towards Diamond Hill. Had the horses been fresh and strong a very severe punishment would have been administered to the enemy; but with weary and jaded animals — many of them miserable Argentines, and all worn out with hard work and scanty food — they were unable to overtake the mass of fugitives who continued to fly before them. A few, however, stood boldly, and one man remained firing his rifle until the charge was close on him, when he shot Lieutenant Wright dead at only a few yards distance, and then, holding up his hands, claimed quarter. This was, however, most properly refused. Altogether ten Boers perished by the lance, and the moral effect on those who escaped must certainly have been considerable. But now in pursuit the regiment gradually came nearer to the enemy's main position, and drew a heavy fire on their left flank.

Seeing this, and having attained the object with which he had charged — the immediate relief of the guns — Lord Airlie gave the orders "files about", and withdrew his regiment before it became too seriously involved. As he issued this command he was struck by a heavy bullet through the body, and died almost immediately. So fell, while directing his regiment in successful action, an officer of high and noble qualities, trusted by his superiors, beloved by his friends, and honoured by the men he left. The scanty squadrons returned in excellent order to the positions they had won, having lost in the charge, and mostly in the retirement, two officers, seventeen men, including a private of the 10th Hussars, who managed to join in, and about thirty horses.

Meanwhile the pressure on Broadwood's right had become very severe. A large force of Boers who were already engaging in the 17th Lancers and the rest of Gordon's Brigade, but who were apparently doubtful of attacking, seeing the advance checked, now swooped down and occupied a kraal and some grassy ridges whence they could bring a heavy enfilading fire to bear. Broadwood, who throughout these emergencies preserved his usual impassive composure, and whose second horse had been shot under him, ordered the Household Cavalry to "Clear them out."

The troopers began immediately to dismount with their carbines and the General had to send a second message to them, saying that it was no good firing now, and that they must charge with the sword. Whereon, delighted at this unlooked-for, unhoped-for opportunity, the Life Guardsmen scrambled back into their saddles, thrust their hated carbines into the buckets, and drawing their long swords, galloped straight at the enemy. The Boers, who in this part of the field considerably outnumbered the cavalry, might very easily have inflicted severe loss on them. But so formidable was the aspect of these tall horsemen, cheering and flogging their gaunt horses with the flat of their swords, that they did not abide, and running to their mounts fled in cowardly haste, so that, though eighteen horses were shot, the Household Cavalry sustained no loss in men.

These two charges, and the earnest fashion in which they were delivered, completely restored the situation; but though Broadwood maintained all the ground he had won, he did not feel himself strong enough, in face of the severe opposition evidently to be encountered, to force his way through the poort.

At about noon the Field Marshal, who was with the Eleventh Division, observing an apparent movement of the enemy in his front, concluded that they were about to retreat, and not wishing to sacrifice previous lives if the strategic object were attained without, sent Ian Hamilton a message not, unless the resistance of the enemy was severe, to weary his men and horses by going too far. Hamilton, however, had seen how closely Broadwood was engaged, and fearing that if he stood idle the enemy would concentrate their whole strength on his Cavalry commander, he felt bound to make an attack on the enemy on the lower slopes of Diamond Hill, and so hold out a hand to Broadwood.

He therefore directed Bruce-Hamilton to advance with the Twenty-first Brigade. This officer, bold both as a man and as a gen-

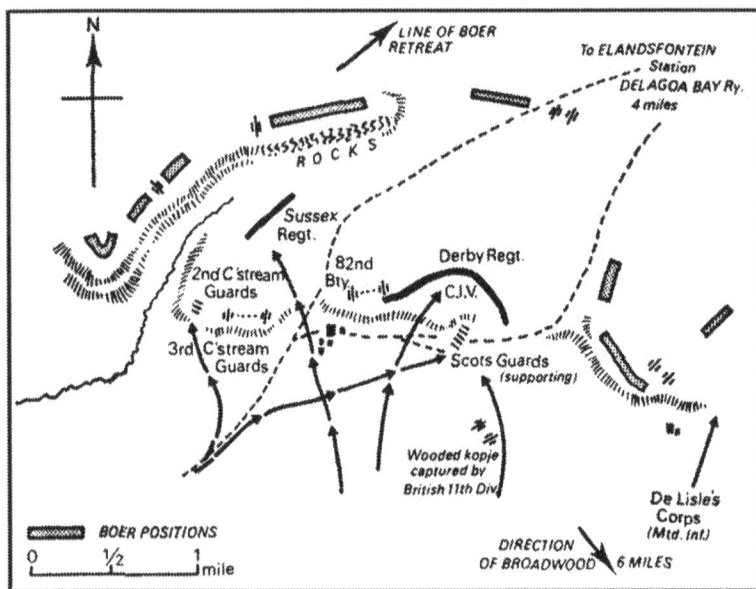

THE ACTION OF DIAMOND HILL

eral, immediately set his battalions in motion. The enemy occupied a long scrub-covered rocky ridge below the main line of hill, and were in considerable force. Both batteries of artillery and the two 5-in. guns came into action about two o'clock. The Sussex Regiment, moving forward, established themselves on the northern end of the ridge, which was well prepared by shelling, and while the City Imperial Volunteers and some parts of the Mounted Infantry, including the Corps of Gillies, held them in front, gradually pressed them out of it by rolling up their right.

There is no doubt that our Infantry have profited by the lessons of this war. The widely-extended lines of skirmishers moving forward, almost invisible against the brown grass of the plain, and taking advantage of every scrape of cover, presented no target to the Boer fire. And once they had gained the right of the ridge it was very difficult for the enemy to remain.

Accordingly at 3.30 the Boers in twenties and thirties began to abandon their position. Before they could reach the main hill, however, they had to cross a patch of open ground, and in so doing they were exposed to a heavy rifle fire at 1,200 yards from the troops who were holding the front.

From where I lay, on the left of the Gillies' firing line, I could see the bullets knocking up the dust all round the retreating horsemen, while figures clinging to saddles or supported by their comrades, and riderless horses, showed that some at least of the bullets had struck better things than earth. So soon as they reached fresh cover, the Dutchmen immediately reopened fire, and two of the Gillies were wounded about this time.

The City Imperial Volunteers then occupied the whole of the wooded ridge. One poor little boy, scarcely fourteen years old, was found shot through the head, but still living, and his father, a very respectable-looking man, who, is spite of his orders from the field cornet, had refused to leave his son, was captured; but with these exception the Boers had removed their wounded and made good their retreat to the main position. It being now nearly dark the action was broken off, and having strongly picketed the ground they had won, the infantry returned to their waggons for the night.

It was now imperative to carry the matter through, and in view of the unexpected obstinacy of enemy, the Field-Marshal directed Pole-Carew to support Hamilton with the brigade of Guards in his attack the next day.

Early the next morning Hamilton's infantry moved forward and re-occupied the whole of the ground picketed the previous night. On the right De Lisle's corps of mounted infantry prepared to attack; the cavalry maintained their wedge-like position, and exchanged shots all along their front with the Boers; but no serous operations were begun during the morning, it being thought better to await the arrival, or, at least, the approach, of the brigade which had been promised.

During this interval the Boers shelled our batteries heavily with their long range 30-pounder guns, and General Ian Hamilton, who was siting on the ground with his Staff near the 82nd Field Battery, was struck by a shrapnel bullet on the left shoulder. Fortunately, the missile did not penetrate, but only caused a severe bruise with numbness and pain, which did not, however, make it necessary for him to leave the field. The case of this shell, which struck close by, ran twirling along the ground like a rabbit — a very peculiar sight, the like of which I have never seen before.

At one o'clock the leading battalion of the Guards was observed to be about four miles off, and Bruce-Hamilton's Brigade was therefore directed to attack. The Derbyshire Regiment, which had been briskly engaged during the morning, advanced up a flat tongue of land on the right. The City Imperial Volunteers moved forward in the centre, and the Sussex on the British left. Though this advance was exposed to a disagreeable enfilade fire from the Boer "pom-pom", the dispersed formation minimised the losses, and lodgments were effected all along the rim of the plateau. But once the troops had arrived here the fight assumed a very different complexion.

The top of the Diamond Hill plateau was swept by fire from a long rocky kopje about 1,800 yards distance from the edge, and was, moreover, partially enfiladed from the enemy's position on the right. The musketry immediately became loud and the fighting severe. The City Imperial Volunteers in the centre began to suffer loss, and had not the surface of the ground been strewn with stones, which afforded good cover, many would have been killed and wounded. Though it was not humanly possible to know from below what the ground on top of the hill was like — we were now being drawn into a regular rat-trap. It was quite evident that to press the attack to an assault at this point would involve very heavy loss of life, and, as the reader will see by looking at the rough plan I have made, the troops would become more and more exposed to enfilade and cross-fire in proportion as they advanced.

After what I had seen in Natal the idea of bringing guns up on to the plateau to support the Infantry attack when at so close a range from the enemy's position seemed a very unpleasant one. But General Bruce-Hamilton did not hesitate, and at half-past three the

82nd Field Battery, having been dragged to the summit, came into action against the Boers on the rocky ridge at a distance of only 1,700 yards.

This thrusting forward of the guns undoubtedly settled the action. The result of their fire was immediately apparent. The bullets, which had hitherto been whistling through the air at the rate of perhaps fifteen or twenty to the minute, and which had compelled us all to lie close behind protecting stones, now greatly diminished, and it was possible to walk about with comparative immunity. But the battery which had reduced the fire, by keeping the enemy's heads down, drew most of what was left on themselves. Ten horses were shot in the moment of unlimbering, and during the two hours they remained in action, in spite of the protection afforded by the guns and waggons, a quarter of the gunners were hit. Nevertheless, the remainder continued to serve their pieces with machine-line precision, and displayed a composure and devotion which won them the unstinted admiration of all who saw the action.

About four o'clock General Ian Hamilton came himself to the top of the plateau, and orders were then given for the Coldstream Guards to prolong the line to the left, and for the Scots Guards to come into action in support of the right. Two more batteries were also brought forward, and the British musketry and artillery being now in great volume, the Boer fire was brought under control. Ian Hamilton did not choose to make the great sacrifices which would accompany an assault, however, nor did his brigadier suggest that one should be delivered, and the combatants therefore remained facing each other at the distance of about a mile, both sides firing heavily with musketry and artillery, until the sun sank and darkness set in.

General Pole-Carew, who with the Eighteenth Brigade was still responsible for containing the Boer centre across the railway, now rode over to Hamilton's force, and plans were made for the next day. It must have been a strange experience for these two young commanders, who, fifteen years ago, had served together as aides-de-camp on Lord Roberts's staff, to find themselves together now under the same chief designing a great action as lieutenant-generals. It was decided that Hamilton's force should move further to the right and attack on the front, which, on the 12th, had been occupied by De Lisle's corps of Mounted Infantry, that the Brigade of Guards should take over the ground which the Twenty-first Brigade had won and were picketing, and that the Eighteenth Brigade, which was now to be brought up, should prolong the line to the left. But these expectations of a general action on the morrow were fortunately disappointed. Worsted in the fire fight, with three parts of their positions already captured, and with the lodgment effected by Colonel De Lisle's corps on the left threatening their line of retreat, the Boers shrank from renewing the conflict.

During the night they retreated in good order from the whole length of the position which they occupied, and marched eastward along the railway in four long columns. When morning broke and the silence proclaimed the British the victors, Hamilton, in order to carry out his original orders, marched northward and struck the railway at Elandsfrontein station, where he halted. The mounted infantry and cavalry were hurried on in pursuit, but so exhausted were their horses that they did not overtake the enemy.

Such were the operations of the 11th, 12th, and 13th of June, by which, at a cost of about 200 officers and men, the country round Pretoria for forty miles was cleared of the Boers, and a heavy blow dealt to the most powerful force that still keeps the field in the Transvaal.

After the action of Diamond Hill the whole army returned to Pretoria, leaving only a mounted infantry corps to hold the positions they had won to the eastward. French and Pole-Carew, whose troops had marched far and fought often, were given a much-needed rest. Ian Hamilton, whose force had marched further and fought more than either, was soon sent off on his travels again. The military exigencies forbade all relaxation, and only three days' breathing space was given to the lean Infantry and the exhausted horses. By the unbroken success of his strategy Lord Roberts had laid the Boer Republicans low. We had seized the heart at Bloemfontein, the brain at Pretoria. The greater part of the railways, the veins and nerves, the trunk still quivered convulsively, particularly the left leg, which, being heavily booted, had already struck us several painful and unexpected blows.

To make an end tow operations were necessary: first, to secure the dangerous limb, and, secondly, to place a strangling grip on the windpipe somewhere near Komati Poort. The second will, perhaps, be the business of Sir Redvers Buller and the glorious Army of Natal. The first set Hamilton's Brigades in motion as part of an intricate and comprehensive scheme, which arranged for the permanent garrisoning of Frankfort, Heilbron, Lindley, and Senekal, and directed a simultaneous movement against Christiaan De Wet by four strong flying columns.

I had determined to return to England; but it was with mixed feelings that I watched the departure of the gallant column in whose good company I had marched so many miles and seen such successful fights. Their road led them past Lord Roberts's headquarters, and the old Field-Marshall came out himself to see them off. First the two cavalry brigades marched past. They were brigades no longer; the Household Cavalry Regiment was scarcely fifty strong: in all there were not a thousand sabres. Then Ridley's brigade of nearly 5,000; thirty guns dragged by skinny horses; the two trusty 5-inch "cow-guns" behind their teams of toiling oxen; Bruce-Hamilton's Infantry Brigade, with the City Imperial Volunteers, striding along — weary of war, but cheered by the hopes of peace, and quite determined to see the matter out; lastly, miles of transport: all streamed by, grew faint in the choking red dust, and vanished through the gap in the southern line of hills. May they all come safely home.

APPENDIX

COMPOSITION OF LIEUT.-GENERAL
IAN HAMILITON'S FORCE

DIVISIONAL STAFF

LIEUTENANT-GENERAL IAN HAMILTON, C.B., D.S.O.

A.D.C.s — Captain de Heriez Smith.
    Captain Balfour, late 11th Hussars.
    Captain Maddocks, R.A.
    Captain Duke of Marlborough, I. Y.
A.A.G. — Lieu.-General Le Gallais, 8th Hussars.
D.A.A.G.s — Captain Vallentin, Somerset, L. I.
    Captain Gamble, Lincoln Regiment.
    Captain Atcherley, A.S.C.
    Captain Kirkpatrick, R.E.
Provost Marshall — Captain Sloman, East Surrey Regiment.
Div. Signalling Officer — Captain Ross, Norfolk Regiment.
P.M.O. — Colonel Williams, N.S. Wales A.M.C.
Divisional Troops — Rimington's Guides under Major Rimington,
    Inniskilling Dragoons.

2nd MOUNTED INFANTRY BRIGADE

BRIGADIER-GENERAL R. RIDLEY

A.D.C. — Captain Hood, Coldstream Guards.
Brigade Major — Lieut.-Colonel Mitford, East Surrey Regiment.
Staff Officers — Captain Sir. R. MacMahon, Royal Welsh Fusiliers.
    Captain Eustace Crawley, 12th Lancers.

2nd MOUNTED INFANTRY CORPS

Lieut.-Colonel de Lisle, Commanding Durham Light Infantry.

Staff Officer — Captain Fanshawe, Oxford, L. I.
6th M. I. Battalion — Captain Pennefather, Welsh Regiment.
New South Wales Mounted Rifles.
West Australians.
1 Pom-pom.

5th MOUNTED INFANTRY CORPS.

Lieut.-Colonel Dawson, I.S. C.

Staff Officer — Captain Ballard, Norfolk Regiment.
5th M.I. Battalion — Major Lean, Warwick Regiment.
Roberts' Horse — Captain Baumgartner, East Lancashire Regiment.
Marshall's Horse — Captain Corbett.
Ceylon M. I. — Major Rutherford.
1 Pom-pom.

6th MOUNTED INFANTRY CORPS

Lieut.-Colonel Legge, 20 Hussars.

Staff Officer — Captain Hart, East Surrey Regiment.
7th M.I. Battalion — Major Dobell.
Kitchener's Horse — Major Cookson, I.S.C.
Lovat's Scouts — Major A. Murray.
1 Pom-pom.

7th MOUNTED INFANTRY CORPS

Lieut.-Colonel Bainbridge, Buffs.

Staff Officer — Captain Hamilton, Oxford, L.I.
7th M.I. Battalion — Major Welch.
Burmah M.I. — Captain Copeman.
1 Pom-pom.

P. BATTERY

Ammunition Column — Major Mercer, R.H.A.
Bearer Company and Field Hospital — New South Wales Army
 Medical Corps.

2ND CAVALRY BRIGADE

BRIGADIER-GENERAL BROADWOOD

A.D.C. — Captain Aldridge, R.H.A.
Brigade Major — Captain Hon. T. Brand, 10th Hussars.
Signalling Officer — Captain Sloane Stanley, 12th Lancers.
Household Cavalry — Lieut.-Colonel Calley.
10th Lancers — Lieut.-Colonel Fisher.
12th Lancers — Lieut.-Colonel Earl of Airlie.
Q. Battery, R.A.
Ammunition Column — Captain Kincaid, R.A.
Bearer Company.
Field Hospital.

19th BRIGADE
MAJOR-GENERAL SMITH-DORRIEN

A.D.C.s — Captain Hood, R.M.L.I.
 Lieut. Dorrien Smith, Shropshire, L.I.
Brigade Major — Major Inglefield, East Yorkshire Regiment.
76th Battery — Major Campbell.
1st Royal Sussex — Lieut.-Colonel Donne.
1st Derby — Major Gossett.
1st Cameron — Lieut.-Colonel Kennedy.
City Imperial Volunteers — Brigadier-Colonel Mac-Kinnon; Colonel the Earl of Albermarle.
Bearer Company.
Field Hospital.

DIVISIONAL ARTILLERY
LIEUT.-COLONEL WALDRON, R. F.A.

81st Battery.
82nd Battery — Major Conolly.
1 section of Five-inch gun — Captain Massey.
Ammunition Column — Captain Hardman.

EFFECTIVE FIGHTING STRENGTH

11,000 Men.
4,600 Horses.
8,000 Mules.
36 Field guns.
2 Five-inch guns.
23 Machine guns.
6 Pom-poms.

The force left Bloemfontein, April 22.
Arrived at Pretoria on June 5.
Distance traversed, 401 miles in a straight line.
Time on the march, 45 days.
Halts, 10 days.

General actions on nine days:
 Israel's Poort, April 25.
 Houtnek, April 30 and May 1.
 Welkom, May 4.
 Sand River, May 10.
 Affair of Lindley, May 20.
 Doornkop (Florida) May 29.
 Six Mile Spruit (Pretoria), June 4.
 Diamond Hill, June 11 and 12.

Eighteen days' skirmishes.

Towns captured:
    Thabanchu.
    Winburg.
    Ventersburg.
    Kroonstadt.
    Lindley.
    Heilbron.
    Johannesburg.
    Pretoria.

www.ingramcontent.com/pod-product-compliance
Lightning Source LLC
Chambersburg PA
CBHW021232090426
42740CB00006B/489